DR. WYATT FISHER

Total Marriage Refresh: 6 steps to marital satisfaction

First edition

ISBN: 9798696209456

This book was professionally typeset on Reedsy.
Find out more at reedsy.com

I dedicate this book to my wife Alia. So thankful we've made it through to the other side. I love you!

Contents

Preface

Falling in love is easy, but staying in love is difficult, hence the 50 percent divorce rate. What happens to all those couples gazing lovingly into their partner's eyes at the altar? No one signs up for marriage and spends thousands of dollars for a wedding only to get divorced one day. Obviously, cracking the code on marriage is the quest of a lifetime, and this book is designed to get us further along that quest. I'm Dr. Wyatt Fisher. I was born and raised in Ohio until I was about six years old, when my parents got a divorce. A few years later, my mother remarried, and we moved to Colorado with my new stepdad and stepbrother. Then, at age fifteen, I moved to Texas to live with my biological father and stepmother.

My upbringing was tumultuous, to say the least. Blended families can be extremely difficult, and I experienced intense valleys common in broken families. However, through those valleys, a desire rose in my heart to help. I wanted to make a difference and help families stay together. So, as I went through undergrad and into graduate school, I felt a tug on my heart toward marriage counseling. My credentials include a master's and doctorate in clinical psychology and I'm a licensed psychologist in the state of Colorado. I've also been in private practice since 2004, where I specialize in marriage counseling. On a personal note, I've been married since 1999.

Instead of having an idyllic marriage, I have had a very challenging one, for a variety of factors I'll explain as we walk through the chapters in this book. I'll sum it up by saying wounds in both of our backgrounds crippled our development as a couple, and we've had to work really hard to get to where we are today. On the bright side, my marital challenges have profoundly increased my insight into helping other couples and compassion for how difficult marriage can be. Therefore, I write this book not as an expert who has all the answers but as someone who has been through the valleys and is journeying alongside you on the matrimony trail.

One interesting thing to consider is how much time, money, and energy most people invest into their careers compared to their marriages. The difference is staggering. At my Total Marriage Refresh conferences, I often ask couples how many years they went through vocational education and training, and the majority raise their hand with two to four years. However, when I ask how many people have gone through at least six months of marital education and training, no one raises their hand. No wonder marriage can be so difficult; we haven't been trained on how to do it right! My hope is that this book will provide you with essential marriage training, probably much overdue training that's desperately needed.

Another thing to consider is this book will have a different impact on each one of you. Good marriages require two things: the right kind of heart and the right kind of tools. If you have the right kind of heart but lack marital tools, your relationship will struggle. Likewise, if you have the right kind of marital tools but lack the right kind of heart, your relationship will struggle. Both are needed! This book will provide a tremendous number of marital tools. However, they won't be effective unless you have the right kind of heart, which is someone who is open to new insights, reflective, takes ownership for their part, and is motivated to improve. In addition, the level of difficulty you're facing in your relationship now will probably impact how much help you still need after reading this book. For some of you, this book will provide a tune-up with a minor to moderate course correction for your marriage. For others of you, grappling with deep problems and resentments in your marriage, this book may be just the beginning to your healing journey. So, where your relationship is before reading this book will most likely impact where you'll be after reading it. The book also won't cover every possible topic on marriage. If it did, it would end up being thousands of pages long! However, it will cover concepts and strategies that can be applied to virtually any topic on marriage. In addition, the majority of case studies and examples shared in the book are on heterosexual couples because that's who I've seen the most in my private practice. However, the principles covered are applicable to all relationships, whether heterosexual or homosexual.

The pages ahead will walk you through the top six steps needed for long-lasting marital satisfaction. The steps must go in order to maximize results. If you jump around in the steps, you won't experience optimal benefits because each step builds upon successfully establishing the previous one. I developed these six steps out of years of working with couples in my private practice, marital research, and experiences from my own marriage. I'm convinced the six marriage steps can turn any marriage into true happiness. The steps, if followed, will transform your relationship into the best it's ever been! You'll also notice there are multiple application questions and exercises throughout each chapter. Be sure to do them all, because content is internalized deeper if it's discussed and practiced instead of passively read about. Last, don't rush. Take your time reading the concepts in this book and let them soak in so they can change you from the inside out.

Let's begin.

Chapter 1

Marriage Step One: Establishing a Covenant Foundation

Most people know the divorce rate is around 50 percent for all first-time marriages. However, most people don't know it's often higher for subsequent ones. This is usually because people in their second and third marriages used divorce as an option in their past, so it's easy to use again. Gone are the days where divorced people are frowned upon as a social outcast. Now, divorce is everywhere, and most of us have family members or friends who have been divorced, or we have ourselves. Because it's so common, it often seems like a perfectly reasonable solution to marital problems. Divorce has become normalized. Therefore, it readily comes to our minds as a possible solution when we hit a rough patch in our marriage.

Another factor encouraging divorce is the upgrade culture we live in. We continually are bombarded with advertisements telling us to upgrade to the newest phone, laptop, TV, car, etc. Without realizing it, we often take this upgrade mentality over into our marriage. If we aren't happy with our spouse, why not upgrade and get a better model? Changing out what we have for something better often seems like the solution, even in marriage.

From these reasons and countless others, divorce has become a central part of our social fabric, whether we like it or not. Obviously, none of us got married hoping to get divorced one day. Why would anyone spend thousands upon thousands of dollars for wedding dresses, rehearsal dinners, and reception halls, only to get divorced? They wouldn't. Virtually everyone getting married believes it's the best decision they can make, and they can't wait to begin their married life together. However, as joy turns to strain, divorce readily becomes an option for many couples.

One thing to consider is all the reasons *not* to get divorced. First, divorce can emotionally cripple and debilitate children. Their entire world falls apart, and their sense of security is shaken. Children do best with stability and predictability, and divorce turns their world upside down. Children and teens of divorced homes often struggle in their development, because instead of focusing on their own growth, they become preoccupied with their family stress. In addition, divorce models for your children what to do when they go through difficult times in their marriage one day. Second, divorce is extremely expensive, usually costing you half of everything you own. That is substantial! Is getting a divorce worth losing half of everything you have worked so hard for? In addition, you will also need to pay alimony if you have children, which makes things even more expensive. A friend of mine was stressed because of his unhappy marriage, so he pursued a divorce, but now he is stressed from the $5,000 he pays his ex-wife each month for child support. So, his overall stress has stayed the same, but now he is much poorer! Having said all that, there is a time and place for divorce, which I will discuss later. However, many times, couples rush to divorce before really thinking through the consequences and before really trying to salvage their relationship.

All marriages go through seasons

According to Gary Chapman (2012) all marriages go through seasons, just like our weather patterns. Summer is the first season, where things are hot outside and the trees and grass are thriving. Likewise, in relationships, summer is when couples first begin dating and are madly in love. They are extremely attracted to one another, can only see the good in one another, and want to continually spend time together and share every detail of their lives. However, just as summer gives way to fall and the weather gets cooler, relationships tend to cool off after the first eighteen months. This usually is when couples get married and first move in together and they've been together long enough for the newness of the relationship to fade.

Usually around this time, conflict starts to enter in, needs stop being met consistently, hidden resentments start to build up, and imperfections in your partner become more visible. If couples aren't careful during fall and address their slow drift in the wrong direction, they can easily slip right into winter. Just like our weather, winter is cold and frigid. If you step on a fallen branch during winter, it easily breaks, and this is when many couples break. Winter is when the in-love feelings are gone, resentment is entrenched, and needs are not being met. Most couples get divorced in this season if they are unable to resolve their differences. However, for those who dig deeper during this phase and receive needed support, they can make it through and go right into spring. During spring the trees start to bud, the birds start to chirp again, and there's a new warmth in the air. Likewise, with relationships. This is when couples start falling back in love again, start resolving their resentments, and begin meeting one another's needs, perhaps better than ever.

The point of these seasons is to recognize that all couples go through them. It's normal! Therefore, when your marriage cycles through the seasons, you know all couples experience it. Unfortunately, many couples enter marriage with the misconception that their relationship will stay in summer forever. Then, when they hit fall and winter, they make false conclusions, such as "I must have married the wrong person" or "My needs are never going to be met in this marriage" or "I'm never going to be happy in this relationship." These false conclusions often lead to divorce. In contrast, couples who are cognizant of these seasons can form different conclusions when they slide into fall and winter, such as "We are in winter; all couples go through this," or "We're in winter; we need to work harder at our relationship and get some help." The benefit of recognizing the seasons is you'll respond better to them when they occur.

Application Question:

What season do you feel your marriage is in right now and why? (Don't be alarmed if you think you're in one season and your spouse thinks you're in a different one. That's normal, and the whole point of this book is to begin discussing topics you usually don't.)

Your marriage is alive

The next concept to consider is that your marriage is alive. I'm a gardener, and I love getting my hands in the dirt. I read a book many years ago, before we bought our first home, on edible landscaping, and I developed a vision of being able to walk through my yard and have a meal by popping some berries here and some vegetables there. I haven't come close to accomplishing that vision yet, but each house we've moved into, I've gone crazy planting as many things as I could. We've lived in our current house since 2008, and I've planted close to twenty-five fruit bushes and trees so far. With all that experience planting, I've learned over and over how much living organisms take intentional effort to thrive. They need a certain amount of light, a certain amount of water, and a certain type of soil. If the conditions aren't right, they wilt and die. Marriage is the exact same way: it needs a certain amount of light, a certain amount of water, and a certain type of soil to thrive. If we are intentional, we can nurture it to health; however, if we neglect it, it will wilt and die.

I work with couples in my practice who had thriving marriages for decades; then something happened, and they took their focus off their relationship, and it wilted and started to die. If I put a plant under my desk where it couldn't get water and light, it wouldn't last long before it suffered, and that's exactly what most of us do to our marriage. We neglect it, and then we're surprised when it wilts and dies. Most of us gave our relationship all of our attention in the beginning, when we were falling in love, but after marriage our attention often turns outward to careers, finances, kids, etc., and our marriage suffers as a result. So, what would your marriage look like if it were a plant? Would it be beautiful, green, and thriving, or would it be wilted, brown, and dying?

Application Exercise:

If you think of your relationship as a living organism, what sun, water, and fertilizer does it need to get healthier? Fill in the next chart.

Sun, Water, Fertilizer Options	***Check off the ones you feel your marriage needs most and discuss how you could implement it.***
Daily time to talk	
Regular dates	
More affection/sexual connection	
Learn to work through conflicts effectively	
More compliments	
What else?	

Contract vs. covenant marriages

Chapter 1

There are two approaches to marriage, the contract and the covenant. The contract is most relationships today and is entirely based on feelings. It says *I'm committed to you as long as my needs are met, I'm in love, and I'm happy. However, the moment you stop meeting my needs, I'm not in love with you anymore, or I'm not happy, divorce becomes a viable option.* You know this is most marriages in our culture today because those are the reasons you hear for divorce. There's nothing wrong with feeling deeply satisfied in marriage. In fact, that's the ultimate goal of marriage this book will help you achieve. However, when our commitment is 100 percent contingent on our feelings, our marital union becomes fragile because feelings ebb and flow.

In contrast, the covenant marriage is based on principle and says *I'm committed to you despite having seasons of winter when my needs aren't met, I'm not in love, and I'm not happy.* Covenant couples sign up for the long haul, through sickness and health, for richer or for poorer. It's a covenant you're making with your partner lifelong. The only exceptions in a covenant marriage where divorce is permissible are the three A's: adultery, abuse, and abandonment. Also, if a top need of yours is continually expressed, and your partner refuses to work on it or improve, this would qualify as neglect, which falls under the abuse umbrella. In these situations, marriage counseling is recommended to explore and resolve the impasse. Perhaps your partner has unhealed trauma blocking them from meeting your needs. Perhaps you're doing things that are making it difficult for them to meet your needs. If they are still resistant and dismissive of your needs after three to six months of marriage counseling, then a separation is recommended. A separation sends the message *I still love you, and I want our marriage to work; however, ignoring and dismissing my needs is unacceptable.*

Deciding how you're going to approach marriage is critical, because it will greatly impact how you approach problems. If you're in a contract marriage and go through a winter season, one foot will already be out the door considering divorce. However, if you're in a covenant marriage and go through winter and the three A's aren't occurring, then you know divorce isn't an option. The only option is to dig deeper and try harder. I've gone through this in my marriage several times. We've been through seasons of winter where I wasn't happy and everything in me wanted a divorce. However, because the three A's weren't occurring, I knew divorce wasn't an option, so I had to dig deeper and try harder to make it to spring, and eventually we did. If I would have approached my marriage as a contract, I'd be divorced right now.

A major advantage of the covenant approach is that it breeds security. If you know your partner is in it for the long haul, you'll feel more secure in the relationship. Increased security leads to greater vulnerability, which leads to greater emotional and sexual intimacy. In contrast, if your partner frequently throws out divorce as a threat, that will create insecurity in the relationship, which will lead to less emotional and sexual intimacy.

Application Questions:

What impact would it make if you approached your marriage as a covenant rather than a contract?

How could you move in that direction?

Marriage is the ultimate refining tool

Chapter 1

Nobody likes to suffer and experience strife. However, challenges are inevitable in marriage because it involves two imperfect people living together day in and day out. Therefore, sparks are going to fly. When they fly, it's critical to consider how you may be getting refined through the challenges. Just as jewelers heat up gold so the imperfections can rise to the surface to be removed, the same is true in marriage. When things heat up in marriage, our shortcomings are often highlighted so we can work on them to get better. This perspective provides purpose in the pain. For example, perhaps the current friction in your relationship is revealing how you tend to be self-absorbed, defensive, too independent, critical, contemptuous, etc. Therefore, one of the best questions to ask yourself the next time you're upset with your spouse is "What does it say about me that I'm upset with them about that?"

Marriage is one of the most powerful refinement tools to make us better versions of ourselves, if we allow it. We can fight against our spouse's constructive feedback and resist it, or we can see their criticism as an opportunity to become a better person and partner. This is another benefit to the long-term covenant approach to marriage: we can be refined. In contrast, if we jump from relationship to relationship, we bring all our baggage with us and never change. One area my marriage has refined me in is learning to become more considerate. Many years ago, when we only had two boys who were ages three and one, my wife and I decided it was time to plan our first family vacation. So, I decided to spearhead the idea by taking charge. First, I went online to look for cabins in the mountains. Before long, I got impatient with all the details of the results, so I booked the first one that looked good, without researching it thoroughly for reviews, amenities, etc. Next, I went to a bike store to purchase a bike rack so my wife and I could take our new bikes with us on the trip. At the store, I found the bike rack section and briefly browsed the various models. I found the cheapest one, and without asking for any recommendations from the employees, I purchased it and headed home.

Once home, I started getting the bikes ready for the trip as my wife packed the car. I hate reading directions, so I threw out the bike rack manual and proceeded to put it on the back of the car to the best of my ability, which isn't saying very much. Next, we piled into the car and proceeded to drive toward Glenwood Springs, Colorado along I-70, cruising at around eighty miles an hour. Every twenty to thirty minutes, I looked back to make sure both bikes were okay, and so far, so good. We finally reached our exit after about three hours of driving, and we exited to the right and stopped at a light. While stopped, I decided to glance back at the bikes one more time, and when I did, there was only one bike instead of two! I quickly hopped out of the car and ran to the back to double check, and sure enough we were missing my wife's bike. I couldn't believe it. I dropped off my wife and kids at the cabin and drove back thirty miles, thinking I would find my wife's bike, but I never did. Understandably, she was very disappointed to lose her new bike, all because I hadn't taken the time to get a quality bike rack and taken the time to properly install it.

Then, as we slept that night in the cabin, starting around 9:00 p.m., bright lights started shining through our windows. I went out to see what it was and realized our cabin was right next to a truck stop. Therefore, all night we had large trucks pulling in and shining their lights into our cabin, making sleep nearly impossible. If I would have been more thorough in my research and read the reviews of the cabin, I would have known this.

The last disaster of the trip, which wasn't my fault, was with my oldest son, Forrest. There was a little creek running down the middle of our camping area with six cabins on each side. Little did we know, Forrest had been playing with the rocks on the side of the creek and dislodged so many of them that the water overflowed the banks and flooded all the cabins. We reported it to the office, and they quickly brought a crew to come re-dig the borders of the creek to stop the flooding. Phew, what a first vacation! It certainly taught me lessons on the importance of becoming more considerate in my decision-making and how it impacts my family.

Application Exercise:

What are the top ways your marital challenges are making you into a better person? Fill in the next chart.

Possible areas of refinement from marital challenges	***Check off all that apply and discuss how the challenges in your marriage are making you better at each one.***
Becoming more patient	
Becoming a better listener	
Becoming more selfless	
Becoming more of a team player	
Learning to take responsibility for my part in conflict	
What else?	

Application Question:

What parts of the chapter were most helpful for you and why?

References

Chapman, Gary (2012). *The Four Seasons of Marriage.* Tyndale House Publishers.

Chapter 2

Marriage Step Two: Owning Your Brokenness

We often hear we are to become one in marriage. However, learning to become one can be difficult, especially when dealing with two imperfect people. Becoming one applies to spirit, soul, and body. Becoming one spiritually refers to a couple's beliefs, values, and worldview. The more they share the same beliefs, values, and worldview, the stronger spiritual oneness they have. Becoming one on the soul level refers to couples who are best friends. These couples love spending time together and regularly share all their thoughts and feelings. Becoming one on the body level refers to everything physical. These couples enjoy both warm affection and sexual activity, and physical connection is a regular part of their relationship. It's important to note most couples are strong in at least one of the three areas naturally, and they can usually depend on that area to help them through difficult times in their marriage. For example, couples who are strong in body oneness will often rely on their affection and sexual activity during times of marital distress to stay connected. They may be fighting like cats and dogs but are still able to have great sex, and that connection may be the only thing that keeps them together during difficult times.

In my marriage, my wife and I have always been strong in soul oneness. When we first started dating back in 1995, I was a sophomore and she was a freshman at the University of Colorado at Boulder. We fell in love with one another quickly and knew early on we wanted to get married one day. Shortly after our explosive beginning, we started a habit of writing our thoughts down while we were going to class and studying. The thoughts we wrote down were anything we were thinking or feeling throughout the day. We would then meet up each night and pull out our pieces of paper and "share our thoughts." The habit stuck because we've done it almost every day since! Even now, with four children under seventeen, we prioritize our talk time each night for around an hour before going to bed.

While that has been our strength, the body oneness has been our biggest struggle. Unfortunately, my wife experienced sexual trauma growing up, which left her with beliefs like "sex is dirty, sex and love do not go together, and I have no voice with sex." Starting on our wedding night, we could tell something was definitely wrong. While I couldn't wait to consummate our marriage, it was the last thing on her mind. Facing sexual activity became highly anxiety-inducing for her because of her traumatic past, making her avoid it. The more she avoided it, the more rejected I felt. Instead of tenderly expressing my feelings of rejection, I responded with anger. The angrier I became, the more unsafe I seemed to her so she avoided sex even further, making me feel even more rejected. This created a toxic, vicious cycle in our relationship for years. To make matters worse, at the time I was just beginning graduate school in psychology so I thought I could be our therapist. Big mistake! You never can be your own marriage therapist because you're not objective. However, I was determined to fix us so I refused seeking help. This massive misstep led us into years of misery until we were both hanging on by a thread. Feeling completely hopeless, we finally reached out for help. Thankfully, that slowly began our healing journey over several years working with multiple trauma therapists as we unpacked our vicious cycles and healed the resentments it had created for both of us.

Application Questions:

What area of oneness is strongest for you in your marriage (body, soul, or spirit), and which is your weakest and why?

What could make your weakest area better?

Defining brokenness

This chapter is all about brokenness and understanding its role in marriage. Brokenness refers to the culmination of all the shortcomings and weaknesses both you and your spouse have. Your brokenness was probably present before entering your marriage. Your spouse had nothing to do with it. Then, your areas of brokenness interacted with your partner's, and vicious cycles developed. We tend to be good at pointing out the shortcomings in our spouse but fail to recognize our own. One helpful tip to remember is whenever you are pointing your finger toward your spouse, you have three fingers pointing back at yourself. This chapter will help you identify your areas of brokenness and how they impact your marriage. To own your brokenness means you know what they are, and you can list them off without excuses. One of the top benefits to owning your brokenness is you'll be able to resolve conflicts much faster. For example, if you know you tend to be critical and that's an area of weakness for you, you'll be much faster to sift through conflicts to discern if you were being critical and apologize if you were. If you are out of touch with your shortcomings—or worse, don't think you have any—it will be virtually impossible to resolve conflicts with you because you won't ever see your part.

Chapter 2

Case Study: Jennifer and Jon were a couple I saw in my practice. Jennifer was very controlling and short-tempered. The two traits went hand in hand because when she would begin to lose control, she became verbally aggressive to regain control. Unfortunately, she couldn't identify and own these areas of brokenness, which left Jon continually hurt, frustrated, and disillusioned. Whenever they had conflicts, he was able to stay calm and articulate his frustrations, then take ownership for his part. However, she would lose her temper, become controlling, and never circle back to take ownership for her bent and apologize. Her narrative was Jon was causing the conflicts, without any insight into her own contribution to them. Over several years of this pattern, they grew more and more distant as a couple because their conflicts drove a wedge between them. When they finally started working with me, one of the first things I did was help them identify and own their brokenness. While Jennifer was resistant at first, she slowly was able to acknowledge her bent to be controlling and short-tempered. Once this occurred, their conflicts changed. For the first time, she could see her contribution to their fights and apologize for her part, which helped their reconciliation and marriage tremendously.

Owning your brokenness creates emotional safety and humility that becomes grease in the wheels of your marriage. When both partners are humble enough to own their brokenness, tenderness and forgiveness follows. One light-hearted example of brokenness in my life is that I'm not handy with repairs around the house. I've gotten better through the years, but it's certainly not my natural strength. My wife and I bought our first residence in Virginia Beach in 2000. It was a condo in foreclosure, so we got a super deal. Little did we know it was right next door to a drug dealer! Therefore, we had people coming to our house at all hours of the night thinking we were the drug dealers. One night scared my wife, as a man continually banged on our door demanding to get paid. Thankfully, he eventually left, and the next day, I decided to help my wife feel safe and purchased a heavy-duty lock for our front door. I bought one that attached to the top of the door with a metal loop that attached to the doorframe. There I was, inside of our house installing the new lock and feeling proud of myself. I noticed the screws included only could be tightened but not loosened, which I had never seen. Finally, I finished and went to open the door from inside our house to test the lock and realized I had installed it backwards and locked us into our house. The door wouldn't open! Because I couldn't loosen the screws, I had to use a crowbar to pull off the wood trim around the door where the lock was installed. So much for being a reliable handyman for my wife!

The next week, my wife asked me to install some blinds on our windows that faced the parking lot, so we could have more privacy. I measured the window openings first, which I was impressed with myself for doing, and off to the hardware store I went. I bought the blinds and came home ready to install them. I opened the box and slid out the blinds and noticed there was a set of strings wrapped around them. I thought to myself, "the strings must be for keeping the blinds together in the box," so I took some scissors and cut right through them, not realizing those were the strings for the blinds! I then went to install the blinds in the brackets in the window and all the blinds fell right to the floor. My wife certainly wasn't impressed with my abilities. Being lousy at home repairs is an area of brokenness for me.

Chapter 2

The need for transparency

A great question for all of us to ask is, "What would it be like to live on the other side of me?" Consider your moods; are you joyful or crabby? Consider your energy; are you lethargic or hyper? Consider your habits; are you organized or sloppy? Consider your words; are you a pessimist or optimist? Considering what it would be like to live on the other side of you can be humbling. Often, we are so consumed with how difficult it is to live on the other side of our partner we never consider what it would be like to live on the other side of us. We all wrestle with brokenness on some level. It's part of how we are wired. We each have tremendous talents and strengths but also areas of weakness and flaws. Our brokenness is involuntary.

It takes strength to admit our weaknesses. What are yours? Anybody can act perfect and pretend they have it all together. You hear this often in conversation. "Hey John, how's it going?" "I'm doing good, yep, everything is great." These types of interactions don't breed connection, they breed isolation. It doesn't mean you need to share your struggles with everyone. However, we all need one or two people in our lives to become fully transparent with about who we really are and what we are struggling with. Most people don't have these types of relationships, and they walk around in isolation with the most vulnerable parts of who they are because they fear being judged. True strength is taking the risk to open up and share who we really are and what we're really feeling, warts and all. Owning our brokenness is built upon a covenant foundation because lifelong commitment creates security. Security creates safety, and safety creates fertile ground to share the ugliest parts of who we are, our brokenness.

Case Study: Megan and Matt were a couple in my practice who had been married for several decades. They had grown children and successful careers. However, they had developed a lot of problems in their marriage over the years. One of their knots they needed help untangling was the pattern of the husband always getting defensive and acting like he was flawless. Understandably, this infuriated the wife, making her feel continually invalidated and alone. One day in session, I pulled out my white board and introduced the idea of brokenness to them and how it's a vital element to a healthy marriage. We proceeded to list the top three areas of brokenness for the wife and then for the husband. He struggled at first identifying what his were, but the wife was happy to help, as you can imagine! Once the list was created, he was able to finally see and own his tendency to do all three areas on his side of the board, giving the wife a huge surge of emotional release. Finally, she felt validated. Finally, she felt like an equal partner instead of inferior. Finally, she felt respectful toward her husband for admitting and owning his brokenness.

Kintsugi

As you may or may not realize, your partner is in the best position to provide feedback on your shortcomings. In no other relationship are you with someone day in and day out, in close proximity for them to observe all aspects of who you are. However, hardly anyone ever asks their partner what shortcomings they see in them. I always ask couples at my Total Marriage Refresh conferences to raise their hand if they have ever asked their partner what shortcomings they see in them, and no one raises their hand. Because we don't ask that question, our partner gets fed up with our flaws and points them out, often rudely. Imagine regularly asking your partner what your growth areas are and then working at improving them. That in and of itself could transform your relationship! Modeling that level of courage and humility to receive feedback would inspire your partner to do the same. Our partner's feedback on our shortcomings is an asset because we all have blind spots. Your spouse can provide objective feedback that no one else can, so use it to grow! In Asia they have a practice called *Kintsugi,* where they glue broken pots together with gold resin. Therefore, a broken pot becomes more attractive and valuable than a perfect pot. We are the same. When we identify and own our brokenness, we become more attractive to our spouse compared to when we act like we're flawless. When we own our brokenness, we create a safe environment for our partner to do the same.

Brokenness chart tool

My wife's areas of brokenness	My areas of brokenness
Defensive	Critical
Two eyes in	Stonewalling
Passive	Controlling

Now I'm going to discuss the top three areas of brokenness my wife and I have, so you can understand how this works. The first one for my wife is she tends to get defensive. This stems from her feeling inadequate growing up. As a child she often felt unimportant, and the feeling continued into early adulthood. If someone doesn't feel good about themselves, it can be difficult for them to receive constructive feedback, which makes them defensive. Another weakness for her is she can be two eyes in, where she loses track of my life because she's so focused on hers. She had an insecure attachment growing up, so it turned her inward for survival. A third shortcoming for her is a tendency to be passive. Her passivity stems from rarely feeling like her voice mattered growing up. Since our marriage in 1999, she has grown tremendously in all three areas, but she still tends to slide in these directions if she's not careful.

One of my areas of weakness is I can be critical. Growing up, I was told what I was doing wrong rather bluntly. Therefore, my natural bent when I'm upset is to do the same. If I'm not careful with how I express myself, I can sound critical. Another weakness of mine is stonewalling. Stonewalling is where someone refuses to talk when they are upset. Growing up, my mom would tell me I was in the doghouse when she was upset and not speak to me. When I get upset I tend to do the same where I shut down and refuse to talk. A third weakness of mine is I can be controlling. I tell people I'm a control freak in recovery. A control freak is someone who likes things a certain way, and they think their way is *the* way. That's me. I tend to be very particular with all sorts of things in my life. This is from both my genetics and environment growing up. My mom and dad were both constantly cleaning and organizing things and I was always required to help. Our weekends were filled with cutting the grass, washing the cars, cleaning the toilets, etc. Everything had to be just right. Obsessive-compulsive personality traits run in my family, which is connected to a need for mastery and control in one's environment. However, it took me a while to realize there was also an emotional component to my controlling bent. I was always the skinny kid growing up and several times I was the target of bullying. I can remember riding my bike away from those experiences with tears running down my cheeks, vowing to never be powerless again. Gaining power and control was a way to feel safe so I would never feel weak again. Unfortunately, I took this bent right into my marriage, which was a big mistake and something I've really had to work on. Like my wife, I have improved in my three areas of brokenness tremendously since being married, but they still can get the best of me if I'm not careful.

Application Exercise

Common areas of brokenness include:

Critical

Defensive

Controlling

Unreliable

Poor listener

Two eyes in

Passive

Too independent

Secretive

Selfish

Decide who will be Partner A or B, pick your top three areas of weakness, then ask your spouse if they agree or disagree with your list and why. Would they change any of them?

Remember your partner is in the best position to give you objective feedback on your growth areas.

Also, remember not to get defensive but view their feedback as an opportunity to become a better person and partner.

Next, explain to your partner what you experienced growing up that may have contributed to your brokenness areas.

Partner A's areas of brokenness	**Partner B's areas of brokenness**

Another important component to the brokenness chart is to search for the vicious cycles. Most conflicts in marriage arise out of both partners' shortcomings interacting and creating vicious cycles. Therefore, the brokenness chart will probably explain the majority of all your conflicts and why you have them. For example, if I'm expressing my frustrations to my wife with criticism, it's going to encourage her to get defensive because she feels attacked. The more she gets defensive, the more critical I become because I feel like she isn't taking responsibility for her part. The more critical I become, the more defensive she gets. On and on it goes. Another example is if my wife is being passive, it fuels my control-freak bent to take over. The more I take over, the more passive she becomes because she feels I want things my way. The more passive she becomes, the more frustrated I get, because I feel like I must do it all and I take over even more. On and on it goes.

Application Questions:

What are the vicious cycles that develop between both of your areas of brokenness? Draw a line between those areas on the chart you filled out.

How could recognizing your vicious cycles benefit your relationship?

Strengths

While this chapter intentionally focuses on the shortcomings of both partners in marriage, it's also important to remember the strengths. To keep a healthy perspective, you need to be mindful of both you and your spouse's strengths and weaknesses. If all you know are your strengths and your spouse's weaknesses, you'll feel superior. If all you know are your weaknesses and your spouse's strengths, you'll feel inferior. Therefore, being mindful of both you and your partner's strengths and weaknesses is key. So, let's spend a few moment looking at the good stuff.

Application Exercise

Common areas of strengths include:

Thoughtful

High Integrity

Hard Worker

Great With Kids

Humorous

Great Listener

Loving

Great At Compromising

Decide who will be Partner A or B, then fill in the chart below on your partner's top three strengths and discuss what you love most about each one.

Partner A's Strengths	Partner B's Strengths

Bullseye question tool

Now let's put all this together into an effective tool. We need a regular way to provide feedback to our partner on two things. First, we need a safe way to discuss things they've done that has hurt our feelings or upset us. But how do we share such information? Most of the time, we avoid sharing complaints because we don't want to start a fight. However, when we bottle up our feelings we either become snarky or we pull away emotionally. Both are unhealthy. We need a way to share complaints easily before they build into resentments, which we'll cover more in chapter four. Second, we also need help looking for the good in our partner and what they did right because our human nature makes us look for the bad. Looking for the good will make us feel more positive toward our partner, it will make them feel good to hear it, and it will encourage them to do more of it. The bullseye question tool is the solution. Once a day, get in the habit of asking your partner, "What's one thing I did right today and what's one thing I could have done better?" The main ground rule when receiving feedback is you're not allowed to get defensive. If you defend yourself in response to the feedback then your partner will avoid giving it to you. However, you can ask clarifying questions if you're confused on the feedback. The main thing to say in response is "thank you for the feedback." Then, mull over the feedback on your own for the next day or so and search for the piece of truth in it that you can work on for improvement. This simple tool can be transformational for couples by giving them a daily, safe space to express complaints and focus on the good.

Application Exercise

Pause now and take turns asking one another the bullseye question "What's one thing I did right today and what's one thing I could have done better?" Remember to follow the ground rule!

Application Question:

What parts of the chapter were most helpful for you and why?

Chapter 3

Marriage Step Three: Learning to Share Power

It's been said when two people become one in marriage, the trouble starts when they try to decide which one. Partners, some more than others, have a natural desire to make their spouse into themselves. They'll think, "If only my partner were more organized like me, more even-tempered like me, more sociable like me, etc., things would be so much better." And off they go, trying to mold their partner into mini versions of themselves. Not surprisingly, this often makes their spouse feel judged and not accepted for how they are wired. David Keirsey (2006) says even though we can never transform our spouses into us, we continually try to anyway, and doing so sends the critical message we want them other than they are. Does this mean we should never expect our spouse to change some of their behaviors to honor our preferences? Certainly not! Part of the wonderful design of marriage is for both partners to sharpen one another through gentle, honest feedback on growth areas, so both can become better human beings. However, if we overdo it by delivering feedback harshly or too often our comments turn into nagging criticism. At the core, we all want to feel fully known and fully accepted in marriage, blemishes and all.

Five keys to acceptance

1. Reframe irritating behavior

Famous marriage researcher John Gottman (2015) says happily married couples learn to view their partner's difficult behaviors as amusing parts of who they are. Think about all the energy you waste dwelling on the parts of your spouse you wish were different. Imagine reframing those parts into amusing characteristics of who they are. One example in my marriage is my wife tends to leave about 20 percent of a task unfinished. She'll get 80 percent through and then stop. Since I'm a control freak by nature and love things to be organized, this bent of hers irritates me. A common scenario is she'll clean the kitchen and do everything except for all the dirty pots left in the sink. I'll walk into the kitchen, and instead of commenting on the 80 percent she did do, I comment on the 20 percent she didn't do. Big mistake! So, to reframe this behavior into an amusing part of who she is, I began referring to it as the 80 percent rule, which has helped me be less aggravated and more accepting of it.

2. Origins of the behavior

The second step to accepting your partner's irritating trait is to reflect on what made them that way. When I thought about my wife's 80 percent rule, I realized quickly it came from her mother. Whenever her mom comes to visit, she leaves piles everywhere! She'll clean up the kitchen or a room about 80 percent and leave the rest clumped together. This is what my wife saw growing up, so it's her normal. Who am I to say my way of organizing 100 percent is the right way? It's important to remember in marriage you're always grappling with two partners' backgrounds filled with subjective definitions of what's normal.

3. Silver lining of the behavior

Search for the silver lining in their aggravating trait. For example, with my wife's 80 percent rule, it's helped me loosen up and not be so obsessive-compulsive with organization. It's forced me to relax my standards of perfection, which has been good for me.

4. Other positive qualities

What are your partner's other positive qualities? We can get so hyper-focused on our spouse's shortcomings; we lose sight of all their positive qualities. One enormous, positive quality my wife possesses is she's one of the sweetest, most tender-hearted people you'll ever meet. She's very slow to judge and abounds in grace. Her tender heart is one of the main reasons I fell in love with her many years ago. Countless people have shared how safe she makes them feel. However, instead of dwelling on this wonderful trait of hers, I hyper-focus on her 80 percent rule and how annoying it is. We lose perspective! Couples who regularly express appreciation for one another tend to have happier marriages. Sometimes, looking for the good in life and in our partner needs to be cultivated. One way to nurture an attitude of gratitude is to spend time each day reflecting on the top things you love most about your spouse. Our feelings and behaviors follow our thoughts. Therefore, intentionally focusing on your partner's positive qualities will make you feel and act more positive toward them too. Another great idea is to start a gratitude journal and put it in a central location like your kitchen table. Then, make it a habit to enter one thing every day you appreciated about your spouse over the past twenty-four hours. What a powerful heirloom for your kids!

5. Your shortcomings

Think about your shortcomings that would be hard for your spouse to live with. Refer to the previous chapter on owning your brokenness for a reminder on your top three areas of brokenness. We are often so zeroed in on our spouse's difficult behaviors we forget what it would be like to live with ours. One example for me is I can be impulsive at times. This came out in my marriage in 2009, when I finally became a licensed psychologist. Becoming a licensed psychologist is a very long and arduous road. It requires four years of undergraduate school, five years of graduate school, then two to four years of postdoctoral hours before you can take the licensure exam. The licensure exam requires at least six months of preparation because it covers everything in the doctoral program. I was extremely nervous and thought for sure I failed the exam because it was so hard. Much to my surprise, I passed. All my hard work and dedication had paid off.

It was time to celebrate, and I felt like I deserved a reward. I came up with the perfect idea: I deserved a sports car! I've had a love affair with cars as long as I can remember, especially sports cars. However, I never owned one and finally felt like my time had come. I tried my best to present my case to my wife with how I deserved a sports car. Unfortunately, she quickly shook her head and said it was a bad idea. "We have four kids, and most sports cars don't have a back seat. Also, we live in Colorado, with ice and snow, and sports cars are rear-wheel drive," she said. Feeling deflated at her reaction, the next day I decided to drive around to some dealerships just to "browse." Tip, never browse for something if you know your partner is not on board. Driving around Denver, I saw a promising dealership, so I pulled in and began looking around. As I stepped into the showroom, there in front of me was the most beautiful piece of craftsmanship I had ever laid eyes on. The color, the curves, and the feel of the car were amazing! As a bonus, it was a convertible with low miles and was being sold for a great price.

I quickly called my wife to tell her about the amazing dream car that was calling my name loud and clear. She reminded me of all the reasons it was a bad idea, but at the end of the call she said, "I'll let you decide." As I hung up the phone the only thing I remembered her saying was "I'll let you decide." Tip, if your spouse is against a purchase then says, "I'll let you decide," it's code for *you better not*. Not thinking clearly because of my sports car fever, I went immediately to the salesperson and said, "I'll take it!" I'll never forget the rush driving home that night with the top down and bugs flying into my teeth because I couldn't stop smiling. I got home and told my wife the great news. She was immediately upset, and problems with owning the car soon began. The next day she asked if I could take our youngest to the dentist but then realized I couldn't because car seats wouldn't fit. The next week, she needed me to pick up all four kids but then remembered I couldn't because the car didn't have a back seat. Tension was mounting.

Finally, I came up with a solution. I would take my wife out on a fancy date and teach her how to drive the stick shift in the new car. Perhaps that would help her fall in love with the car too. Feeling confident about my plan, I made reservations in Boulder at a nice restaurant, and we proceeded to drive there with her behind the wheel. What I didn't know was Boulder was having a severe ice storm. As we entered Boulder, we began seeing cars spinning out on the side of the road because of the black ice. Just as we were observing this, my wife lost control of the car, and we did three 360s before slamming into the median and coming to an abrupt stop. Thankfully, we weren't going fast enough to get hurt or damage the car. My wife looked at me, and I looked at her, and she didn't have to say a word. I knew I had to get rid of the car. With my tail between my legs, the next day I took the car back to the dealership and traded it in for something more family friendly. I owned the car a total of six weeks. So, that's what it can be like to be married to me at times. I can have moments of impulsivity, and I need to remember that when I'm getting frustrated with my wife's 80 percent rule.

Application Questions:

What's your partner's top behavior that aggravates you?

1. How could you reframe the behavior as an amusing part of who they are (like the 80 percent rule with my wife)?

2. What made them that way? (Think about their early-childhood experiences and what was modeled to them.)

3. What is the silver lining in their aggravating behavior?

4. What are their positive qualities that you tend to overlook?

5. What are your most difficult behaviors they must live with? (Hint, check your areas of brokenness from the last chapter.)

Understanding personality

Minor to moderate behavioral changes are reasonable and even expected in marriage to be a good partner. However, major behavioral changes are unrealistic. Don't think you're going to make your introverted spouse extroverted. However, they can learn how to become more sociable in certain settings. Don't think you're going to make your sloppy spouse a neat freak. However, they can learn how to pick up after themselves better. I have all couples I work with in my practice take a personality assessment, for two reasons. First, it helps couples respect differences in their partner's wiring rather than judge them. Second, it helps them see areas where they may be similar and didn't realize it. One of the leading personality assessments in the field of psychology is called the NEO and includes the Big Five personality traits of extroversion, agreeableness, conscientiousness, neuroticism, and openness to experience. People across the globe possess these five personality traits in varying degrees. Each trait is roughly 50 percent genetic, and the other 50 percent is from our early environmental experiences. As our nature interacts with our nurture, our personality is forged by the time we hit adulthood. However, as we develop through life and our environment shifts, so too can some of our traits.

Application Exercise:

Pause here and search online for a free version of the "NEO Big Five Personality Test" for both you and your partner to take. Once you have the results, continue below.

Each of these five traits are on a continuum where you can score 0 to 100, with 100 being the highest and 0 being the lowest. None of the scores are good or bad; it's your temperament. It is what it is. Also, the accuracy of the results is contingent upon how well you know yourself, because it's a self-report. Therefore, it's recommended to have your partner also fill out the test on how they experience you. Then, you can compare your results with how you see yourself with their results of how they view you, to see where the results line up or differ.

Extroversion

Extroversion rates how much you need to be around other people to replenish and recharge your batteries. Those high in extroversion need to be around people to replenish, and they get energized by activity and excitement. In contrast, someone low in extroversion (an introvert) needs alone time and solitude to replenish. For my wife and me, I scored 95 on extroversion, and she scored 40. In our relationship, I tend to be more of the talker. However, I've learned through the years to not talk more than my wife, because it will start making her feel shut down. Therefore, if I notice I've been talking more than her, I'll quiet down and ask her some questions to open her up. One way the test helped me respect our differences on extroversion was when we went on vacation to Mexico several years ago. The first night there, they had a great band playing with free drinks. Being a 95 on extroversion, I was excited to go dancing and have some drinks. However, my wife being a 40 on extroversion was more interested in going back to our room to decompress and relax. In the past, I would have judged her for this and thought she was being boring. However, that night I felt no judgment because I recognized her lower score on extroversion made her desire some quiet time.

Agreeableness

Agreeableness measures how easily someone gets along with others. Someone high on this scale goes with the flow; they don't rock the boat, they avoid disagreements, and they follow the rules. If you're high on this scale, you may be prone to stuffing down negative feelings to avoid conflict. Stuffing down negative feelings often results in passive-aggressive behavior later. Conversely, someone low in this trait can be disagreeable, opinionated, and very direct. I scored a 55 on this trait, and my wife scored an 81. This is certainly accurate, because my wife is very peaceable and gets along with everyone. However, sometimes she'll have hidden hurts or frustrations that aren't expressed and eventually come out months or years later.

Conscientiousness

Conscientiousness refers to how orderly someone is. Someone high in this trait is very organized, task-oriented, and self-disciplined. They are the control freaks who want things a certain way. Someone low on this scale is very spontaneous, free-spirited, and flexible. I scored an 81 on this scale, and my wife scored a 35.

Neuroticism

Neuroticism refers to how likely someone is to experience

anxiety and/or depression in reaction to environmental stress. High scorers quickly become distressed in reaction to environmental stress, whereas low scorers require a tremendous amount of environmental stress before becoming distressed. I scored a 13 on this scale, and my wife scored a 71. It's common for low scorers to view their high-scoring partner as overly dramatic and for high scorers to view their low-scoring partner as insensitive or uncaring. This dynamic has certainly appeared in our marriage at times both ways.

Openness to Experience

Openness to experience refers to how much someone desires novel experiences. Someone high on this trait craves new adventures, new insights, new ideas, and change. Someone low on this trait craves familiarity, tradition, and predictability, and change is stressful. I scored a 47 on this trait, and my wife scored a 2.

Application Exercise:

Decide who will be partner A or B, then fill in the next chart.

Traits	Partner A's Score	Partner B's Score	How do your scores influence your marriage?
Extroversion			
Agreeableness			
Conscientiousness			
Neuroticism			
Openness to Experience			

What was most helpful for you about the personality test results?

What were your biggest surprises?

How could the results help you respect rather than judge differences with your partner?

Don't judge, just honor

It's amazing how much we judge our partner's preferences and needs because we view them through our lens. If they have the same preferences and needs as us, we agree to honor them. If they have different preferences and needs, we often scoff and dismiss them. A perfect example of this in my marriage is the dishwasher. As I'm sure most of you also have, our silverware rack has a plastic grid that can be placed down or up. If you put it up all silverware can be thrown in together. If you place it down, the silverware must be entered into individual slots, preventing the utensils from touching one another so they get cleaner. My wife is more hygiene conscious than I am, and she prefers the grid to be down so the silverware isn't touching during the wash cycle. She says it's not good for the spoons to be spooning! I, on the other hand, think the silverware gets cleaned well enough when the grid is up, and I prefer it because it's faster to load. So, whenever I loaded the dishwasher, she would ask that I put the grid down, and I would think to myself, *That's stupid, and it slows me down,* so I wouldn't do it. The next day, she would unload the dishwasher and see the silverware grid wasn't down and would get frustrated. Again, she would ask me the next time to put the grid down, and I would dismiss her request and think, *She should just be thankful I'm loading the dishwasher instead of being picky with how I'm loading it.* In turn, she would feel voiceless and get upset. Finally, one day I realized how much I was judging and dismissing her preferences and doing things my way instead. I also realized doing it her way would make her feel honored. So, from that day forward I decided to follow her preference and put the grid down before loading the silverware. Immediately, she felt respected, and the new way only took me thirty seconds. Now I do it like that every time and never think twice about it!

This example can be very common. Spouse A expresses a preference or need to spouse B, and spouse B judges and dismisses the request because it doesn't line up with their preferences or needs. Consequently, spouse A feels dismissed and disrespected. The answer sounds simple and obvious, but so many of us don't do it: honor your spouse's requests! Listen to their preferences and do it. Stop judging their needs and honor them, as long as they don't cause you to suffer or make you uncomfortable. When we take our personal judgment toward our partner's preferences out, it frees us to honor them. Are you selfless and considerate toward your partner? Or do you judge and dismiss their requests, like I did with the dishwasher example? When we do whatever pleases us and disregard our partner's input, we aren't sharing power. Sharing power happens when both spouses feel like their voices are heard and their preferences are considered. How much does your partner feel like you listen to them? Do they feel like their voice matters in your relationship? Or do they feel voiceless? John Gottman (2015) says spouses who feel like they don't have a voice because their partner won't listen to them have harsher startups to conflict and desire sex less often. Makes sense. If you don't feel like your partner listens to you or considers your input, it's going to make you upset. The more upset you get, the harsher you'll begin conflicts, and the less sexual desire you'll feel toward your spouse.

Case Study: Jared and Sue were a couple I worked with for a few months in my private practice several years ago. They had been married around ten years and had several children together. Unfortunately, Jared believed he was to be the head of the home, and that entailed making all decisions pertaining to their finances, housing, and day-to-day activities, with or without his wife's consent. Not surprisingly, his wife felt completely voiceless and powerless in the relationship. When she would express her discontent at not being able to influence her husband's decisions, he would become defensive and say she wasn't appreciating his leadership for their family. The more I tried convincing Jared of the importance of his wife having a voice, the more he pushed back. The cycle worsened, and his wife started having emotional outbursts (harsh startups) toward Jared, from feeling so powerless in their decision-making. Instead of Jared seeing her behavior as the result of him not sharing power, he saw her meltdowns as a character flaw. Unfortunately, by the time the couple saw me, this cycle was too deeply entrenched, and the marriage ended shortly after.

Marriage therapist Willard Harley (2013) says the goal for couples is to reach enthusiastic agreement on all decisions that impact their relationship. The word *enthusiastic* is key because couples may reach agreement, but it's usually not enthusiastic agreement. A lot of couples have one partner who is more domineering and wants things their way and another partner who is more passive and gives in. This dynamic can be frustrating for both. The domineering partner can feel frustrated because they want their partner to be more direct and vocal about what they want. The passive partner can feel frustrated because their voice is ignored and dismissed. Therefore, reaching enthusiastic agreement can be a growth area for many couples. The dominant spouse needs to back off and allow space for their partner to speak up, and the passive spouse needs to learn to directly say what they would prefer. If the couple is not in enthusiastic agreement on a decision, they should not move forward until they are. If they reach an impasse, they may need to pull in a trusted family member, friend, or therapist to help them generate more ideas that could be a win-win. The bottom line is to not move forward on any decision, big or small, that will impact your marriage until you're both in enthusiastic agreement. If you move forward before then, resentment will follow. Both partners in a marriage need to feel like equals and like their voice counts on all topics pertaining to the relationship. This is marriage step number three for a reason. Partners will more likely feel like equals if they feel secure through establishing a covenant marriage (Marriage Step #1) and humble through owning their brokenness (Marriage Step #2).

Often, one's upbringing can impact how easy or difficult it is to share power in marriage. For example, someone raised with a permissive parent, where they were allowed to do as they pleased, will usually have a harder time sharing power in marriage because they are used to having things their way. That's me. Growing up with my mom, I was used to doing what I pleased, when I pleased. In contrast, someone raised with a more domineering parent, where they had to submit to their parent, will probably be more passive in marriage and struggle identifying what they think. That's my wife. Growing up, she often felt like her thoughts and preferences were dismissed and overridden. So, I can lean toward not sharing power, and my wife can lean toward giving it up too quickly. Both are unhealthy and dysfunctional. As with most things, the answer is somewhere in the middle, where we learn to both vocalize our preferences while also considering the preferences of our partner.

Application Exercise:

In the next chart, decide who will be partner A or B, then think about who calls the shots in each category. For example, in the financial arena, does partner A or partner B have the final say on how your money is managed, or do you both have an equal voice by sharing power?

Check off the box to indicate who makes the final decisions per category. It's okay if some categories you don't care about, so you let your partner make the decisions, as long as the reverse is true for you in other categories.

At the end of the graph, you want it to reflect roughly 50/50 sharing power. What changes do you need to make to share power more evenly in your relationship?

Area	Partner A	Partner B
Finances		
Child Rearing		
Affection/Sex		
Home Organization		
Hobbies		
Social Life		
Other:		

Bounce the ball tool

One of the best tools to share power I call "bounce the ball." Bounce the ball is where partner A begins by saying their opinion on a topic and the value underlying their position and ends with "What do you think?" then partner B does the same. Saying "What do you think?" is bouncing the ball. In sports, no one likes a ball hog, someone who constantly keeps the ball to themselves and doesn't pass to their teammates. In marriage, when we don't ask for our partner's feedback, we are being a ball hog! In contrast, when both partners are stating their opinion and then saying, "What do you think?" they are being good teammates. After you have expressed your initial opinion and heard your partner's, now you must adjust your position by a few degrees to honor your spouse's position. You then say your new position and end with "What do you think?" Then, your partner must do the same, adjust their position by a few degrees to honor yours and then end with "What do you think?" Eventually, this will lead to a win-win where you both feel good with the decision. As you can see, this technique only works when both spouses are flexible, respectful, and open to influence by their partner.

A recent example where my wife and I bounced the ball is with a blue spruce pine tree in our backyard. This tree is beautiful, but the branches had gotten so long at the base, it was preventing us from walking on one side of our yard. My opinion was we needed to cut all the base branches back to the trunk, and my wife's opinion was we should leave it alone because it was so beautiful. We both stated our opinion and the value under our position and ended with "What do you think?" Her underlying value was the beauty of unaltered nature, and my underlying value was practicality in having an accessible lawn. My wife then suggested a compromise to trim back the base limbs two to three feet to retain the beauty but also provide a walkway around the tree. This was a win-win that we both felt good with because it honored both of our values, and that's what we did. The bounce the ball tool has been a game-changer for us because it's made me more considerate, and it's given a platform for my wife's voice to be heard.

The next chart shows a sample dialogue of a couple using bounce the ball as they discuss technology with their kids.

Partner A	Partner B
1. I think the kids should have no tech after school until bedtime, and that comes from my core need to mentor our kids by establishing good boundaries for them. What do you think?	1. I think the kids should have unlimited tech after school until bedtime, and that comes from my core need of autonomy by letting the kids make their own choices. What do you think?
2. All afternoon and night with tech feels like too much to me. How about we allow them one hour of tech. What do you think?	2. Only giving them tech for one hour out of the whole night feels like too little to me. How about we give them three hours. What do you think?
3. Three hours still feels like a lot of tech time to me. How about two hours. What do you think?	3. That would work for me. Okay, so they will be allowed to have tech for two hours after school until bedtime.

Application Exercise:

Think of three decisions you must make over the next few days that will impact your marriage on some level. They can be anything, such as what to have for dinner, how to discipline your child, how to spend your weekend, etc.

Bring up the topics one at a time and practice "bounce the ball." One of you will begin by stating your opinion on the topic and the value underlying your position and end with "What do you think?"

The other spouse will then do the same. Then you each must modify your position by a few degrees to honor your partner's until you reach a win-win you both feel good with.

Application Question:

What parts of the chapter were most helpful for you and why?

References

Gottman, J. M. & Silver, N. (2015). *The Seven Principles for Making Marriage Work.* Harmony.

Harley, W. F., & Chalmers, J. H. (2013). *Surviving an Affair.* Baker Publishing Group.

Keirsey, D., & Bates, M. (2006). *Please Understand Me II: Temperament, Character, Intelligence.* Prometheus Nemesis Book Co.

Chapter 4

Marriage Step Four:
Developing Emotional Attachment

Emotional attachment is the level of emotional closeness a couple experiences. This is marriage step number four because it's difficult to build emotional attachment if the relationship isn't secure through a covenant approach, not emotionally safe because you're not owning your brokenness, and doesn't feel like two equals because you're not sharing power. The level of emotional closeness in a relationship often ebbs and flows depending on a variety of variables. However, there are specific skills that can encourage emotional attachment, regardless of your circumstances and regardless of your bent toward or away from emotional intimacy. As you can imagine, there's a lot to cover on this topic, so let's begin.

Eight tips for emotional closeness

1. Shared meaning

The first tip to cultivate emotional closeness is to engage in shared meaning together (Gottman, 2015). Shared meaning refers to doing something you both believe in. Couples who engage in shared meaning together tend to feel closer to one another. Some examples could include volunteering together, gardening together, remodeling your home together, exercising together, etc. Find something that matters to both of you and do it together often. It will bind your hearts together!

2. Digital boundaries

The second tip to cultivate emotional closeness is to have digital boundaries. Most couples have one partner who's more obsessed with their screen than their partner, and it strains the relationship. It's difficult to feel close with someone who's connecting more with their tech than with you. Does your partner feel like your screen gets more attention than they do? If so, you need to set some digital boundaries. One option is to have a gadget curfew. For example, some couples leave all gadgets outside their bedroom after a certain time each night, so they can provide their undivided attention to one another. This gives them regular time to connect without the interference of texts, calls, or notifications distracting them. Another idea is to have a tech Sabbath where once a week, you go tech free for a certain amount of time to spend quality time with one another. For example, some couples will power down their phones for four to six hours every Sunday so they can enjoy the day together without tech interference. Also, discuss how phones should be handled during meals, dates, vacations, etc. so you're both in agreement. Control your tech; don't let it control you!

3. Active listening

The third tip to cultivate emotional closeness is to practice active listening when your partner is speaking to you. It's ideal to set aside designated talk time each day when the kids are in bed, the TV is off, and there's no distractions. During this "talk time," it's important to practice active listening skills, such as maintaining eye contact, summarizing back what your partner is saying, and empathizing with their feelings. We'll focus more on how to empathize later, but for now, think of it as having your partner's back. Some short empathy reactions to your partner's venting can include, "that sucks," "that sounds stressful," "how horrible," etc. These short, empathy-based comments will make your partner feel that you care and you're on their side. It also will encourage them to open up and share more with you, which is the essence of emotional closeness. When I teach about empathy, I always think of my neighbor Doug. He's a big bodybuilder from another country and has a son named Jack who cries easily. One day Doug was asking me what he should do when his son cries. I suggested he try responding with empathy, such as "It's okay, buddy, that must have hurt." Five minutes later, Jack was in my driveway, and Doug was across the cul-de-sac with his daughter when Jack fell and scraped his knee. As usual, Jack began crying and screaming. Doug heard the screams but was unable to run over because he was taking care of his daughter, so instead, he yelled over to me, "Hey, Wyatt, give Jack some of that empathy." That story always makes me chuckle.

4. Head/heart check tool

The fourth tip to cultivate emotional closeness is to practice a head/heart check at the beginning of the day and again at the end of the day. The head is your agenda, such as appointments you have, tasks you must complete, etc. Most couples already share "head" items because they must coordinate their schedules. Couples rarely, however, share their hearts. The heart refers to what you've been feeling and why. The four main emotional categories are mad, sad, glad, or fear so anything you feel will most likely fall under one of those four. Sometimes your feelings will be connected to your agenda items, and other times they'll be an undercurrent you're feeling that has nothing to do with your agenda. For example, you may have feelings of anxiety because of a season of life you're going through that has nothing to do with your schedule for the day. Some people are really good at identifying and articulating their emotions, while others really struggle with it. If you struggle with it, take some extra time journaling each day on what you're feeling and the possible reasons. Just a few minutes a day reflecting on if you're mad, sad, glad, or fearful and why can be enough to start connecting the dots. The more in touch you become with what you are feeling and the possible causes, the more you'll have to share, which will help your partner feel closer to you.

Think of the head/heart check as two bookends to your day. The first is about five minutes in the morning before you go your separate ways, where you ask one another "What's on your head and heart?" The information shared during this brief morning check gives you things to text your partner about throughout the day to show you care. Then, sometime before bed, follow back up with the items shared in the morning and share anything else from your day. For example, if your partner shared in the morning they felt sad about a recent conflict with a friend, you could follow up on that topic with a question, such as "How are things going with the friend you had a conflict with that you mentioned this morning?"

Sharing what's going on in your life and having your partner follow up about it is one of the top ways to feel known and cared for in marriage. The essence of emotional connection is regularly sharing your inner world with your partner and hearing about theirs. Also, our emotional state is always evolving. What makes you mad, sad, glad, or fearful today may be completely different than what will make you feel those things a month from now, six months from now, or two years from now. We are in constant flux. Therefore, without a daily head/heart check, you'll quickly become outdated on your partner's inner world. One of the loneliest things is when you feel like your partner doesn't know the real you. A final tip to the head/heart check is don't use it to share anything negative you're feeling about the marriage. Otherwise, your partner will start associating it with time to be criticized and avoid it. If you're feeling something negative about your partner, that's a conversation for a different time, using a different skill set, which I'll cover later.

The next chart is an example of a couple doing their head/-heart check.

Partner A	Partner B
1. What is on your head and heart?	1. Things were hectic today with my meetings. On my heart, I felt mad with my boss for overworking us and sad that I do not talk with my mom much anymore.
2. That sounds like a hectic day. Makes sense you would be mad with your boss. I can see how you would be sad that you have not been talking with your mom more recently too.	2. Thanks. What is on your head and heart?
3. My day was uneventful. There is not enough work to keep me busy at my job. On my heart, I felt scared that I may lose my job if this keeps up, and I felt happy that I spent time with my friends.	3. That sucks your day was so slow. I can see how that would make you scared to lose your job. It is great you have such close friends and got to spend time with them last night.

5. No solutions unless asked

A fifth tip to cultivating emotional closeness is never give advice unless asked. This is a massive trap many partners fall into. They hear their partner venting about something difficult in their life, and with the best intentions, they respond with solutions. The venting partner quickly becomes irritated because they didn't want solutions; they wanted support. Many people tend to be "fixers," so in response to their partner venting, they try to fix the problem. However, that's the wrong way to fix. You want to fix your partner's emotional distress, not the problem they are describing. Fixing emotional distress is accomplished through empathy statements, as mentioned previously, such as "that sounds really stressful," "makes sense you would feel that way," etc. Empathy comments show you have their back and you care.

6. Two birds on the same branch

Gottman (2015) suggests the ideal way to respond to your partner venting is to imagine two birds. The first bird is your partner, and they are sitting on their branch, venting about something that upset them. They are discussing what happened and how it made them feel from their vantage point on the branch. You, on the other hand, are on a different branch, listening to them and seeing the situation from your vantage point. Not surprisingly, when your venting partner finishes, you respond with solutions from your vantage point on your branch. This upsets the venting partner because it feels like you're forcing them to come over to your branch. Instead, they want you to fly off your branch and land on theirs and try to see the situation from their perspective. Sitting on their branch and seeing the situation from their vantage point produces empathetic comments that makes them feel cared for, such as "that sucks," "how horrible," "no wonder you feel that way," etc.

Empathy variable tool

Application Exercise:

To develop empathy in your marriage, try the empathy variable tool by asking each other the following questions. Write your partner's answers down and review them frequently so you become more mindful of all the factors influencing their reactions to life, which will deepen your empathy for why they feel certain things.

1. What are the top emotional wounds from your upbringing?

2. What are the top values you were raised with?

3. What are your main personality traits?

4. What are your top insecurities?

5. What are your top stressors?

6. What are your top needs in our marriage?

7. What are your top values in life?

7. Dates and vacations

I recommend carving out two mini dates per week to fully connect with your partner. They can range from one to three hours. Willard Harley (2013) suggests doing four things during quality time together to ensure both partners have a nice time. First, provide a lot of affection (nonsexual touch). Second, do some type of recreational activity you both enjoy, such as biking, hiking, roller blading, board games, etc. Third, cultivate emotional intimacy by doing the head/heart check as discussed earlier. Fourth, do some type of sensual activity, which I'll cover more in the next chapter. If only two or three of the four activities occur, usually one partner will walk away saying it was a great time, and the other will walk away saying it was just okay. Therefore, all four are recommended for both partners to feel like it was a nice time together. All screens should be powered down to provide one another your undivided attention. Watching shows together is okay if it is the minority of time not the majority. This amount of time together may sound unrealistic, but consider how much time you spend surfing the internet, watching shows, doing your hobbies, spending time with friends, etc. You probably have the time; you're just choosing to spend it on other things, and your marriage is suffering as a result. A plant can't thrive without proper sun and water. Quality time together is sun and water for your relationship. On your non mini date days, be sure to provide affection and do the head/heart check to maintain your connection.

When it comes to vacations, have at least two a year together, without children and without other family and friends. If you don't have family nearby to watch your kids, consider swapping with friends who also have kids, so you can return the favor. You need to have special alone time where you get away from the stress of life and give your marriage undivided attention. It's hard to fully unplug in our normal routine. Therefore, getting out of our everyday life and vacationing somewhere provides tremendous freedom to be in the moment and see our partner without a million distractions. It's ideal to have the two vacations roughly six months apart to break them up. One could be a weekend getaway and the other one weeklong. Also, do whatever you can afford in cash. The last thing you need after a nice vacation is stress from debt. The main thing is to get away, not spend a lot of money, unless you're in a financial position to do so.

8. Marriage huddle tool

Another tip is to have a once-a-week marriage huddle. Think

about a football team. Before each play, they huddle to discuss the next play so everyone is on the same page. If a football team never had a huddle, there's no way they would win. Likewise, with couples. They have no chance of becoming a unified front without a weekly huddle. A weekly huddle provides an opportunity for couples to get on the same page on all topics pertinent to their relationship, such as finances, kids, chores, etc. This is the time to share your concerns, share power, and develop strategies per topic you both feel good with. This will build a sense of teamwork and unity in your relationship, so you don't feel alone and divided. The marriage huddle is also an ideal time to go through your love buckets discussed in chapter six.

Application Question:

Which of the eight tips for emotional closeness did you find most helpful, and which ones would you like to implement this week and why?

Emotional bids

Gottman (2015) discusses how partners continually make bids to one another for connection. Bids are different for each person, depending on their top needs. Some top needs may include quality time, emotional intimacy, recreational activity, affection, sex, etc. For example, if someone has a need for quality time, they may make a bid by saying something like "Let's put the kids to bed early tonight so we can have some time together." Or, if their need is emotional intimacy, they may make a bid by saying "I haven't shared what's going on in my world in a while." The first step is recognizing your partner is making a bid. Most spouses are unaware their partner is making a bid and miss it and how you respond to their bids is paramount. Once you recognize your partner's bids, you have three options for how to respond.

First, you can turn away. Turning away is when you hear the bid, such as the example of putting the kids to bed early, and you ignore it by saying, "Can't, I have too much work to do tonight." When you turn away from your partner's bid, it feels very disconnecting and rejecting to them. The second way you can respond to your partner's bid is to turn against, which is the worst. Turning against happens when you become hostile in response to their bid. Following the example above, to put the kids to bed early to connect, the spouse who turns against would respond with, "Can't you see I'm buried in work? All you ever want is to spend time together!" This response will damage your partner because it feels insensitive and harsh. This will make them emotionally withdraw and detach from you. The third option is you can turn toward. Turning toward happens when you recognize your partner is making a bid and you respond positively to it because you know it's important to them. So, with the example of putting the kids to bed early to connect, a partner turning toward would say, "That's a great idea. I have about thirty minutes of work left. Would it be all right if I finished, and then we can have the rest of the night together?" That reaction will make your partner feel honored and loved.

A large part of marital interaction is a continual exchange of bids and responses to the bids. If bids are met with turning toward, it will breed closeness and more bids because they are reinforced. Conversely, if the bids are met with turning away or turning against, it will breed distance and fewer bids because they are extinguished. This concept is very similar to attachment theory in developmental psychology. Attachment theory says the way to cultivate a secure attachment with a child is to continually read their signals and respond sensitively and consistently in meeting their needs (Feldman, 2020). Doing so over time will build trust because the child learns you are safe and will meet his or her needs. Likewise, in marriage, we must cultivate a secure attachment by continually looking for our partner's bids and then turning toward them consistently and sensitively. Doing so will make them feel safe and secure in the marriage.

Application Questions:

What are the top bids your partner makes to you, and what needs to they stem from?

What would it look like for you to turn away, turn against, or turn toward your partner's bids?

Affair recovery

One of the top things that will tear apart any relationship is infidelity. Betrayed partners often develop post-traumatic stress disorder (PTSD) because their entire sense of reality has been lost. PTSD occurs when we lose all control during something traumatic, which is why soldiers in combat and people in natural disasters often develop PTSD. Symptoms of PTSD can include agitation, nightmares, emotional detachment, intrusive thoughts of the trauma, severe anxiety, and many more (Rosenthal, 2017). Roughly half of all couples I see in my practice are there because one of them has had an affair. As you may recall from chapter 1, infidelity is one of the exceptions for covenant marriages where divorce is acceptable. However, if the offending partner takes ownership for their behavior, ends the affair, and is remorseful, recovery is sometimes possible. The path to affair recovery is narrow, and many things can go wrong along the way. However, for those dedicated to healing their marriage it can happen and I've seen many couples do so. The following ten steps are recommended for full affair recovery.

1. End all contact with the lover

This first step is often the hardest. Spouses are usually susceptible to affairs when some of their top needs continually go unmet in marriage. However, deciding to step outside the marriage for an affair is 100 percent the offending partner's decision, regardless of how unhappy they were in their marriage. When someone is unhappy in marriage, it lowers pleasurable chemicals in their brain. Then, someone else comes around and starts meeting their top needs, which drastically increases the pleasurable chemicals in their brain, just like hard drugs do. Therefore, as Willard Harley (2013) points out, an affair becomes identical to a drug addiction because it lights up the same reward center in the brain. So, the problem isn't necessarily the new lover but how they are making the wayward partner feel. Just like with all drug addictions, the goal is to quit cold turkey. If you're addicted to heroin and wanted to quit, you wouldn't continue to take it occasionally, because that would keep you addicted. Likewise, with affairs. If you want to end it, you must never have contact with the new lover again. This may require changing jobs, changing homes, changing friend groups, or even changing cities or states. Whatever it takes. You're vulnerable to falling back into an affair with the person the rest of your life. Once you've been addicted to something, you're always susceptible to falling back into it. Just like weaning off a drug addiction, it often takes around six months for the power of the affair addiction to wear off. Each time you reconnect with the new lover, the six-month timer starts over. The first six months are a very difficult time for both the betrayed spouse and the wayward spouse. The wayward spouse must exercise extreme determination and self-discipline to stay away from their new lover, despite feeling intense desire for them. For the betrayed spouse experiencing PTSD because of the affair, any hint of the wayward spouse reconnecting with their lover retraumatizes them.

Affairs can range from strong emotional attachment with no sexual contact on one end of the spectrum to sexual contact with no emotional attachment on the other. The stronger the emotional attachment, the more of a threat to the marriage. Emotional affairs often develop over a long period of time, allowing both parties to become extremely close and connected. Therefore, ending it is often much more difficult, compared to ending a sexual relationship with little to no emotional attachment. If the cheating partner refuses to end contact with their lover, it's recommended to expose the affair by telling all of your family and friends. Exposure of the affair will often help the wayward spouse snap out of their haze and realize how hurtful they are being. If this doesn't make them stop the affair, the next recommendation is to have a separation from the wayward spouse with zero contact until they are willing to end all contact with their lover. The separation can last up to six months and provides protection to the betrayed spouse from continued emotional abuse of the affair. It also provides the wayward spouse time to experience life without their spouse to determine which way they want to go. If the wayward spouse still refuses to end all contact with their lover after six months of separation, divorce them.

Case Study #1: I worked with Chris and Jen several years ago. Jen continually felt emotionally disconnected from her husband. Despite her many pleas for more emotional intimacy, Chris didn't provide it. With his demanding career and travel schedule, it was hard to find the time. Before long, Jen started conversing with their neighbor, who had plenty of time for her and was an excellent listener. Before long, she started falling in love with him, and it soon turned into a full-blown sexual affair. When I started working with them, she was not remorseful for her behavior and refused to cease contact with her new lover, and Chris refused to require a separation until she did. Unfortunately, this crippled their marriage for years, preventing healing from occurring.

Case Study #2: I also worked with Lara and Don several years ago. Don was feeling continual sexual rejection in his marriage. This undercurrent of disconnection combined with frequent travel created more and more tempting situations with other women. Finally, one night while in a city far away from home, Don gave in and had a one-night stand with a woman he met. When I started working with them in marriage counseling, he was very remorseful, ceased all contact with the new lover, and was willing to do whatever it took to restore the marriage. Though extremely painful for his wife, she was able to slowly work through the affair trauma and give him a second chance. One year later, they were experiencing a better marriage than they ever had in the past because they were both more sensitive and intentional with nurturing their relationship.

2. Open all accounts

After the cheating spouse has stopped all contact with their new lover, it's important to open all accounts for transparency. This includes all social media accounts, phones, emails, etc. The betrayed spouse needs access to all of it to ensure the wayward spouse is not staying in contact with their lover, which is essential to start building back trust. This level of accountability is also necessary to help the wayward spouse break the addiction with their lover. Wrong behavior loves secrecy. Therefore, if everything is out in the open, there's less opportunity to rekindle the romance. Even for couples who have never experienced infidelity, having an open policy with all accounts and passwords is recommended to promote transparency and trust. This step only works if the wayward spouse voluntarily and willingly provides full access to the betrayed spouse rather than the betrayed spouse desperately asking for it. The wayward partner needs to be working much harder than the betrayed partner for full reconciliation to occur.

3. Display heartfelt remorse

It's essential for the wayward spouse to show sincere ownership and remorse for the affair. Unfortunately, many cheating partners feel entitled to the affair because they blame their partner for their marital unhappiness. However, no one makes you cheat. That's your choice. Your partner may have contributed to your unhappiness in the marriage, but it was your decision to violate your marriage vows and develop a relationship with another person. Therefore, you must take ownership for your decision and express sincere remorse for devastating your partner and the foundation of your relationship. If you don't display sincere ownership and remorse for your behavior, it will be nearly impossible for your partner to eventually forgive your actions and move forward.

4. Process through your hurts

As mentioned previously, affairs are one of the most traumatic things for couples to experience. Therefore, there's a lot of hurt that needs to be processed through. Instead of delicately sifting through the hurts, betrayed spouses often turn to harsh anger and rage because of how traumatized they feel. While this may be cathartic, it usually creates even more trauma to the marriage and often pushes the wayward spouse even further toward their lover. Bottling up all the hurt is also toxic and will prevent healing. The wayward spouse also may have hurt feelings around feeling neglected or unhappy in the marriage that needs to be discussed. I teach all couples I work with a conflict-resolution method called the reunite tool, which I'll discuss in detail later. Basically, it's a set of guidelines that keeps conversations on sensitive topics respectful, so both partners feel heard and validated. Couples need to learn a method like the reunite tool and then slowly talk through all their feelings. Because an affair is so traumatic, most couples can't do this step without the help of a trained therapist in the room to ensure the conversation stays constructive.

5. Questions conversation

People often wonder how much detail should be shared about an affair. Some betrayed spouses want to know every detail, while others only want a summary of what happened. Usually the wayward spouse doesn't want to share any details, so the betrayed spouse keeps asking for them, sometimes for years. Each time the affair gets brought up, it retraumatizes the relationship. The betrayed spouse should be the one in charge of how much detail is shared, not the wayward spouse. Therefore, it's recommended for the betrayed spouse to make a list of all the questions they have about the affair and for the wayward spouse to answer them honestly. If their honesty is questionable, some choose to have the wayward spouse answer the questions while connected to a lie-detector test to increase the trustworthiness of their responses. After this conversation, both should agree not to bring up the affair again, so the marriage can start to heal.

6. Managing triggers

Part of post-traumatic stress disorder (PTSD) is getting triggered. Those who have been in combat or natural disasters often experience flashbacks of the horrors they went through. Likewise, those who have been betrayed by an affair will often have flashbacks of the pain they suffered. Therefore, learning how to manage triggers is important for all couples who have experienced infidelity. When triggered, the betrayed spouse must avoid two extremes. The first is not mentioning the trigger and suffering in silence, which will make you withdraw emotionally. The second is becoming verbally assaulting toward your partner, which will lead to bitter conflict. The third and recommended approach is to express each trigger with your tender underbelly. The tender underbelly is the tender feelings underneath your anger, such as sad, hurt, insecure, fearful, etc. For example, a tender underbelly statement when triggered could be "I was watching a movie last night that involved an affair, and it triggered me with the affair and brought up all the feelings of sadness, hurt, and fear." The job of the wayward spouse is to respond with empathy and an apology, such as "I can definitely see how the movie would have triggered your feelings of sadness, hurt, and fear with the affair, and I'm so sorry I hurt you like that." This type of response to triggers creates healing opportunities for the marriage, and if handled constructively, they will occur less frequently with time.

7. Develop compassion

The seventh step is cultivating a deeper understanding of what led to the affair, which often produces compassion. Later in this chapter, I'll explain the steps of the compassion chart, which is a powerful tool to use for resolving resentment. In essence, the compassion chart expands your knowledge of all the variables that were influencing your partner's hurtful behavior toward you. This may include things from their past, things in their circumstances, things you may have been doing, and things in your past that may be getting triggered. The goal is never to absolve your partner of responsibility for the affair; however, it makes a difference when you have a clearer understanding of all the pieces that may have contributed to it. However, you're not going to be in an emotional space to even want to develop compassion unless the previous steps are already in place. Only then will you be willing to work on building compassion. I recommend building compassion around the causes of the affair, instead of trying to forgive it, because forgiveness is often a byproduct of compassion. The more compassion you develop for why they had the affair; the more forgiveness will naturally occur. However, don't rush this step; it is often a step that must be revisited each time the trauma of the affair resurfaces in your mind.

8. Capture and counter your thoughts

Both the betrayed and cheating partner often make interpretations on what the affair means. For example, the betrayed partner may believe "I'm married to a liar" or "If I stay with them, I'm a fool," etc. Conversely, the cheating spouse may believe "I'm a piece of dirt for doing this" or "I'm never worthy of love again," etc. As you can see, these beliefs are absolutes and extremes; therefore, both partners must learn to capture and counter their maladaptive beliefs. One way to do this is through a truth table I cover later in this chapter. In essence, a truth table helps us identify our automatic negative beliefs and then counter them with truth. For example, if a betrayed partner is thinking, "If I stay with them, I'm a fool," they would begin by writing this belief down on paper. Then they would counter the belief with truth, such as "They have ceased all contact with their lover and have shown sincere ownership and remorse, so they are doing all the right things to heal our marriage. A fool would be someone who stays in a marriage if those steps weren't taken." Shifting the belief from an extreme statement that's not accurate to a more balanced one that is will change how you feel and behave because our behaviors and feelings follow our thoughts.

9. Fill up your love buckets

All of us have a love bucket inside of us that must be filled with certain things to help us feel loved and satisfied in our marriage. This is Marriage Step #6 that I'll devote an entire chapter to later in the book. Some common fillers people need to fill their love bucket include affection, emotional connection, sexual activity, etc. In addition, there are certain things that drain our love bucket and make us feel negative toward our partner.

Some common drainers include criticism, stonewalling, feeling voiceless, etc. If you are minoring in the fillers but majoring in the drainers, your partner's love bucket will be extremely low. When love buckets are low, people are at higher risk for affairs because they desperately want their bucket to be full. Again, it's always a choice to have an affair, however, the lower one's love bucket, the more temptation they may feel to have one. Therefore, to lower temptation of future affairs, it's essential to discern what both of you need to fill up your love buckets and what drains them, so you can keep one another's buckets overflowing moving forward.

10. Affair-proof plan

The last step to affair recovery is developing a game plan together on how to affair-proof your relationship moving forward. Most couples never develop a unified strategy on how to minimize their affair risk and then are shocked when their marriage falls into one. This step focuses on specific strategies. For example, "What topics are okay or not okay to discuss with someone beyond your partner? How much should you drink alcohol without your partner there? Is it okay to spend time alone with others you find attractive? If so, how much and when? How should separation through travel be handled to minimize risk? What online activity is and isn't acceptable?" These questions and others are essential for all couples to discuss, especially if there's already been an affair. It's important to come into agreement on these questions, to build a unified front against future infidelity. Remember the goal of reaching "enthusiastic agreement" on all decisions from Marriage Step #3? This list can't be the result of one partner feeling bullied into it, or else it won't stick. The list of boundaries to reduce future affair risk needs to be discussed and negotiated until agreements are made you both feel good with and can fully commit to.

Application Question:

If your marriage has experienced infidelity, which of the ten steps do you need most help with still and why?

Application Exercise:

Discuss together what boundaries you both agree on to reduce the risk of future affairs, and then fill in the next chart.

Behavior	Acceptable	Not acceptable
What topics can be discussed with others?		
What type of touch is okay with others?		
How much alone time can be spent with others?		
How much alcohol can be consumed when apart?		
How should individual travel be handled?		

Truth table tool

The next area that can hinder emotional intimacy is your interpretation of your partner's behavior, which comes from the school of cognitive-behavioral therapy (CBT). CBT says the most important things in our lives are not the events but our *interpretation* of the events. Applied to marriage, we can extrapolate that the most important thing in our relationship is not necessarily how our partner behaves, but our interpretation of their behavior. Think of it in three stages as the ABCs; there's a behavior (antecedent), our interpretation of what that behavior means (behavioral interpretation), and the consequence of how our interpretation makes us feel and behave (consequence). Therefore, how we interpret our partner's behavior needs much attention to ensure it is accurate and not skewed. One of the most common causes of skewed interpretations is unhealed emotional wounds from our past. For example, if a man grew up with a very cold and detached mother and felt unloved, he probably developed an emotional wound of feeling unlovable. Therefore, he may easily interpret his partner's behavior as being unloving, because of his preexisting emotional wound of feeling unlovable. Initially, it can be difficult to discern if our interpretations are accurate or skewed, which is why we must examine them. A tool to do this is what I call the truth table and is adapted from concepts covered in *Mind Over Mood* (Greenberger & Padesky, 2015).

1. Partner's hurtful behavior

You begin by developing a table with four columns. The first column is your partner's hurtful behavior. This can be something they said or did. It's whatever hurt your feelings or offended you. Write it down in this column.

2. Negative automatic thoughts

The second column are your negative automatic thoughts, which are all the things going through your mind in response to your partner's hurtful behavior. These are the interpretations we tell ourselves that our partner's behavior means. This column is typically easy to do because our negative automatic thoughts are well rehearsed. This column is where our trauma lives. The more unhealed emotional wounds we have from our past, the more negative automatic interpretations we'll have in response to our partner's hurtful behavior.

3. Truth

The third column are truth statements that counter each negative automatic thought, if needed. Some of your negative automatic thoughts may be accurate and don't need to be countered, but some may be exaggerated or unfounded, and those need to be balanced with truth. Column three is often the hardest, and most people struggle knowing how to counter their negative automatic thoughts. If you become stuck on this column, it can be helpful to share your negative automatic thoughts with a close friend and see if they agree or disagree with your interpretations of your partner's hurtful behavior. If you're still stuck, it can be helpful to work with a therapist who has expertise in CBT. This is the column I help clients with the most in my practice.

4. Balanced thoughts

The fourth column are balanced thoughts where you combine the negative automatic thoughts with truth statements, connected with "however." There's amazing power in capturing and countering our thoughts with truth! How we think determines how we feel and behave. Once the balanced thoughts have been developed, it's critical to read them daily until they become your new way of thinking, which takes time. Check out the next chart on a man who never felt loved by his mother growing up and how he reacted to his partner not contacting him much during a trip.

1-Hurtful Behavior	**2-Automatic Thoughts**	**3-Truth**	**4-Balanced Thoughts**
My partner and I were separated for two weeks because they were visiting their family, and they barely stayed in contact with me.	1-They do not love me. 2-I am not important to them.	1-We have been married for 20 years, and they always make me feel loved. 2-I know they hate phone calls and become forgetful when traveling.	1-My partner does not love me because they did not stay in contact during their trip; however, we have been married for 20 years and they always make me feel loved. 2-I am not important to them because they did not stay in touch with me during their trip; however, I know they hate phone calls and become forgetful when traveling.

The chart doesn't mean his partner shouldn't become more communicative during their next vacation apart. However, the balanced thoughts column significantly changes how the man is interpreting his partner's behavior, which will change how he feels and behaves. The more unhealed emotional wounds you have from your past, the more the truth table will benefit you. Common emotional wounds from one's past can include feeling powerless, unlovable, like a failure, insignificant, used, shamed, neglected, etc. The stronger your reaction to your partner, the more likely an emotional wound from your past is skewing your interpretation of their behavior.

Here's another example to let the truth table sink in deeper. A thirty-five-year-old female continually has negative reactions toward her partner's sexual desire. Despite her partner's faithfulness and family engagement, she views their sexual desire with hostile suspicion. Consequently, she continually reacts to her partner's sexual advances with anger and thinks they're trying to use her for her body. This continual problem causes them both to retreat from one another emotionally, leading to even less sexual contact. Turns out, this woman experienced severe sexual trauma growing up, and those unhealed wounds are skewing her interpretations of her partner's sexual desire. The next chart could be a truth table for her.

1-Hurtful Behavior	2-Automatic Thoughts	3-Truth	4-Balanced Thoughts
My partner desires sex with me.	1-They are just using me for my body.	1-They have been continually loving and faithful in our relationship.	1-My partner is using me for my body because they desire sex with me; however, they have been continually loving and faithful in our relationship.
	2-Sex is disgusting.	2-It was disgusting to me as a little girl, but between consenting adults it is a beautiful gift.	2-Sex is disgusting; however, it was disgusting to me as a little girl, but between two consenting adults it is a beautiful gift.

Like the previous chart, this doesn't mean her partner doesn't need to work on how they are approaching sex. Perhaps they need to provide more affection or nurture their emotional closeness further. However, it certainly highlights how distorted the woman's interpretations are of her partner's sexual desire, which stems from her unhealed childhood trauma. Obviously, how this woman feels and behaves if she's operating out of her negative automatic thoughts will be vastly different compared to if she's operating out of her balanced thoughts. As mentioned previously, once the balanced thoughts are developed, it's recommended to read them daily until they become your new way of thinking.

Chapter 4

Compassion chart tool

Because marriage involves two imperfect people living in close proximity day in and day out, it's only a matter of time before you hurt your partner or they hurt you, whether intentionally or unintentionally. Mild, unintentional hurts are usually forgotten on their own. However, chronic patterns of hurtful behavior or acute hurtful behavior often builds significant resentment. When resentment enters, intimacy—both emotional and physical—breaks down quickly. Resentment becomes an invisible wall between two partners. When we're hurt, we wall off for self-protection or retaliate to get even, and both are harmful to the relationship. Unhealed resentment is like a weed that takes root that slowly kills the relationship. As you can see, learning how to work through resentment is a major need for couples to have a successful marriage. All too often, well-intending family and friends will encourage forgiveness. "Have you forgiven her? Maybe you just need to forgive him." Forgiveness is often easier said than done and is more of a journey than a destination, because each time the painful memory surfaces, so does the hurt and resentment. Instead of pushing for forgiveness, I encourage couples to work on building compassion toward why their partner hurt them, because forgiveness is often a byproduct of compassion. When compassion grows, forgiveness naturally follows.

If your partner does something hurtful, the first step is to bring it up using the reunite tool, which I'll cover later. A hurtful behavior can be something that hurt your feelings or neglected your top marital needs. If they continue to do the hurtful behavior despite you addressing it several times using the reunite tool, the next step is to seek marriage counseling.

If after three to six months of marriage counseling, your partner still is dismissing and resistant to changing their hurtful behavior, get a separation. Many spouses become complacent in marriage and take their partner for granted. When complacency takes over, hurtful behavior and insensitivity follow. Nothing makes me angrier when working with couples than when I see one partner being indifferent toward their impact on their spouse. They need a wake-up call, and separation often provides one.

The following compassion chart is most effective when working through resentment from previous hurtful behavior your partner is no longer doing. My wife and I fell into a winter season several years ago. She had been a stay-at-home mom for around ten years and was finally developing some great friendships through volunteer activities she felt passionately about. Initially, I was happy for her because it meant so much to her. However, before long she was gone more and more to spend time with her new friends, doing her new volunteer activities. Consequently, I started feeling like a single parent with our four strong-willed children on top of being the only financial provider. I began crumbling under the stress and pressure. Each time I brought this pattern up, she became defensive and wouldn't curb her behavior. In response, my feelings went from hurt to angry to bitter. As we sought help and her behavior eventually changed, the following chart is what I developed to help me sort through my resentment toward her.

Think of a previous hurtful behavior from your partner you still have resentment toward and use it as an example throughout the rest of the chart.

Step One: What about their upbringing may have influenced their hurtful behavior toward you?

When I reflected on my wife's upbringing, I remembered how she was an only child without any extended family around her in Hawaii. In addition, her mother was often gone for extended periods of time for work. Consequently, my wife felt lonely and isolated and would often dream of having a close-knit community of people one day who cared about her. For the first time in her life, she was experiencing that with her new circle of friends. It was filling a hole in her soul.

What about your partner's upbringing may have influenced their hurtful behavior toward you?

Step Two: What about their circumstances may have influenced their hurtful behavior toward you?

When I thought about my wife's circumstances, I thought of how she had been a stay-at-home mom for ten years. While she enjoyed those years, she also felt lost as an individual and isolated. She struggled finding her purpose and value. Now, this new circle of friends and volunteer work were providing both, connection and purpose. Therefore, it was filling a void in her life she had been thirsting for.

What was going on in your partner's circumstances that may have influenced their hurtful behavior toward you?

Step Three: What were you doing, if anything, that may have influenced their hurtful behavior toward you?

After asking my wife for feedback on this, she said I had not been providing much admiration toward her, which is one of her top needs. Somewhere along the lines of being married for several years, raising a family, having a career, and being the sole provider, I had forgotten to make her feel cherished. Therefore, her love bucket was low. However, when she was with her new circle of friends, she received tremendous praise on what a wonderful person she was and how talented she was. She was receiving all the verbal accolades she wasn't receiving at home. So, without realizing it, my lack of praising her at home was contributing to her desire to be gone to receive it.

What were you doing, if anything, that may have influenced your partner's hurtful behavior toward you?

Step Four: What about your upbringing may have influenced how you reacted to your partner's hurtful behavior?

I had a strong reaction to my wife being gone so much, so I started checking in with several of my close friends to see if they felt I was overreacting. By and large, they felt something was off with my wife for her to be gone so much, but they also felt like I was overreacting. This is called a trigger. When your reaction to a situation is stronger than what seems warranted, you're probably being triggered by an emotional wound from your past. When I thought about it, I realized her being gone so much was triggering my trauma from feeling rejected growing up. When I was bullied as a kid, it created intense feelings of rejection, and her behavior was activating that wound. Therefore, I had to acknowledge the issue was not just her behavior, but also my previous wounds were influencing my reaction to her behavior.

What emotional wounds from your past may have influenced how you reacted to your partner's hurtful behavior?

For me, these questions greatly impacted my compassion

toward my wife's hurtful behavior. It helped me recognize her behavior was filling a hole in her soul from her upbringing. Her new circle of friends and volunteer work were making her feel connected and purposeful, she was feeling cherished and praised with her new friends while not receiving it at home, and I was reacting strongly partially because her behavior was triggering my rejection wound growing up. This doesn't mean my wife was totally innocent of her behavior and didn't need to change, but it helped me have more compassion toward her behavior by understanding all the variables that influenced it. As my compassion increased, forgiveness started to follow. It can do the same for you. You owe it to your marriage to work through any lingering resentment you still harbor toward your partner. You won't experience true oneness until you do.

How to manage conflict

The next essential component to developing emotional intimacy centers around successful conflict resolution. You can't feel emotionally close to your partner if you tear each other apart during arguments. Most couples coming to my practice need help with how to manage conflicts more effectively. Usually, how couples handle conflict will influence their susceptibility to divorce. The more you emotionally wound each other during conflict, the higher your risk for divorce. Therefore, learning how to navigate through the treacherous ground of verbal sparring is essential. We don't need training on how to be nasty and cruel when we're upset; most of us are naturally gifted at it. However, we desperately need training on how to be courteous and respectful when we're upset. This section is the beginning to your training.

Core needs

The first thing to consider in conflicts are your core needs. Instead, most couples get lost in the weeds, which are the details in arguments on what was said and what happened. This type of mind-numbing interaction is pointless, and there's rarely a winner because you're grappling with two people's subjective perception of reality. Instead, couples should pause and reflect on what their core needs are underneath the weeds. Core needs may include the need to feel valued, appreciated, heard, respected, cherished, pursued, secure, united, supported, etc. Our core needs are usually from values we grew up with, so we inherently desire them, or from emotional wounds from our upbringing, because we never received them. For example, a little girl who never felt heard growing up may have an emotional wound from feeling voiceless. Conversely, another little girl growing up may have felt routinely listened to, so it became a value for her. Both girls will enter marriage one day with a strong need to feel heard, even though one is coming from an emotional wound and the other is coming from a value. Therefore, in a conflict with her partner, if she starts feeling voiceless, she may get upset and start bickering over the weeds, but underneath is a core desire to feel heard.

If you pause, identify, and express your core need, it changes the nature of the discussion. The weeds take a back seat, and what becomes more important is finding a win-win that will honor both of your core needs. Take the example of a man who grew up in a home where everyone was expected to work equally hard to care for the house, yard, etc. Now, he's in a marriage where he feels like he does more work overall than his partner, which makes him angry and resentful. However, if he were to pause and identify his core need to feel like a team, it could change his approach. With this insight, he could calmly express his core need to feel like a team and avoid getting critical and destructive with his words. When his partner hears the core need instead of the verbal attacks, they will be more motivated to make changes to honor him.

Case Study: Barb and Jim had been married for more than twenty years and had several young adult children in college. Barb had always been a stay-at-home mom, and Jim had a successful business, and this setup worked well for both of them while the kids were still young. However, now that the kids were older and moving on to college, Jim started feeling fatigued from being the only financial contributor to the family and desired Barb to enter the workforce so he could feel more balance in life and like they were working as a team to support their family. Instead of identifying and expressing this core need, he often became rude and disrespectful toward Barb and criticized her spending habits and fun-filled life. When I started working with them, we immediately started helping Jim identify his core need underneath his anger and sarcasm, and he was eventually able to articulate his need to have more balance in life by working less and his desire to feel like they were working together as a team to help contribute to the family. When Barb heard the core need under his rude behavior, her heart softened, and she became more motivated to make changes to honor his need.

Application Question:

What are some of you and your partner's core needs that undergird your arguments, and where do your needs come from?

Practice identifying and articulating them, and then explore how to meet one another's core needs in ways that will work for both of you.

Situation vs. disposition

The next thing to consider with conflicts is the self-serving bias and the fundamental attribution bias from social psychology. Every behavior we do comes from a blend of both our disposition and our situation. *Disposition* refers to personality qualities, such as insensitive, controlling, passive, forgetful, inconsiderate, poor listener, etc. *Situation* refers to circumstances beyond our control, such as heavy traffic, receiving extra assignments at work, a loud environment making it difficult to hear, etc. The self-serving bias says when we do something that upsets our partner, we over attribute our behavior to our situation and under attribute it to our disposition (Myers & Twenge, 2018). However, the fundamental attribution bias says when our partner does something that upsets us, we do the opposite—we over attribute the behavior to their disposition and under attribute it to their situation (Myers & Twenge, 2018). For example, let's imagine you're making dinner and you text your spouse, who's at work, that it will be ready at 6:00 p.m. Six o'clock comes and goes, and your spouse isn't home. The food is hot and ready to be served, but your partner is not there. You get upset. Finally, at six thirty, they rush into the driveway and through the front door, shouting how they hit every red light on their way home. Now, the partner who made the dinner would think most of the reason their partner was late is because of their disposition (inconsiderate) and the minority is from their situation (red lights). However, the partner who is late thinks the other way around. They believe most of the reason they are late is from their situation (red lights) and the minority of the reason is from their disposition (inconsiderate).

You can imagine what happens next. The one who made the meal comments on their partner's disposition: "You're always so inconsiderate," and the late partner retorts with their situation: "It wasn't my fault. I kept hitting red lights." As with most things, the truth is probably somewhere in the middle. In reality, the late spouse probably lost track of time and didn't leave early enough to get home by six, and then, to make matters worse, kept hitting red lights. So, one way to solve this conflict would be for the partner who made the dinner to place more blame on the situation (red lights) and for the late partner to place more blame on their disposition (inconsiderate). Imagine replaying the scenario and the partner who made the dinner says, "Those red lights can be horrible. They've slowed me down a lot too," and the late partner says, "Actually, I was also being inconsiderate, because I could have left earlier, and I'm sorry." Wow, what a difference that would make!

Application Questions:

Think of the last time you were upset with your partner for something they did. How much were you over attributing their behavior to their disposition and under attributing it to their situation?

What would it look like to increase attribution to their situation?

Conversely, think about the last time your partner was upset with you for something you did. How much were you over attributing your behavior to your situation and under attributing it to your disposition?

What would it look like to increase attribution to your disposition?

Flooding

Flooded means your heart rate is elevated, and you are in fight or flight (Gottman, 2015). Some of us flare up and become verbally aggressive (fight), and others of us shut down and retreat (flight). Both are counterproductive. Usually, one spouse gets into fight mode and the other gets into flight mode, which creates a vicious cycle. The more the fighting spouse pursues, the more the flighting spouse retreats. The more the flighting spouse retreats, the more the fighting spouse pursues. Having a conversation when flooded makes everything worse because couples make harsh comments that are later regretted.

Instead, couples need to take a break to de-flood before continuing the conversation. Some common symptoms to know you're flooded include increased heart rate, tingling, flush with heat, difficulty concentrating, sweaty palms, etc. It's important to tune into your body for your signals so you can tell when you are flooded. It's also important to tune into your partner's signals. If either of you get flooded, say "flooded," then take a break to relax before continuing the conversation. The break to de-flood should be no less than twenty minutes and no longer than twenty-four hours. How long you need to de-flood will vary depending on the intensity of the topic and your flooding pattern.

Not going over twenty-four hours before continuing the conversation is important so de-flooding doesn't turn into an excuse to avoid the topic. The break shouldn't be under twenty minutes because it usually takes at least that long to de-flood. During the de-flood time, intentionally do whatever will lower your heart rate, such as taking a nap, being in nature, listening to music, reading a book, etc. Also, during the de-flood time, be thinking through the complainer steps in the reunite tool covered next.

Reunite tool

It's a matter of time before your partner upsets you. They won't meet your needs, they'll be insensitive, they'll have annoying habits, and the list goes on and on. In addition, it's a matter of time before you upset them for the same reasons. Therefore, learning what to do with negative feelings toward your spouse is imperative. Usually, there are two options. First, you can say nothing. However, if their upsetting behavior is significant, not saying anything will make you withdraw emotionally and physically, or you'll become passive-aggressive by making rude or sarcastic remarks. Second, you can verbally assault them with criticism. However, that approach leads to them getting defensive and counter attacking. Also, criticism won't motivate them to change, because they are too busy defending and counter attacking. It's obvious we need a third way, and it's called the reunite tool. The reunite tool is designed to help you constructively make a complaint in a way that will maximize your partner hearing your concerns and feel motivated to change. Marriage expert John Gottman (2015) points out the first few minutes of a conversation often dictate the rest of the conversation, underscoring the importance of de-flooding and then using the following tool. The reunite tool includes four steps for the person making the complaint and five steps for the person listening to it.

The complainer steps

1. Comment on their improvement

You need to begin with how your partner has improved in the behavior you're upset about. If they haven't improved with the specific behavior, zoom out and consider how their overall attitude has improved toward your concerns. If you still can't find any improvement, you may skip this step, but the reunite tool goes much better if you begin with appreciation and praise on how they have improved in the behavior you want to complain about. For example, I was working with a couple who had been married for ten years and were both in their late fifties. The husband had hurt his wife's feelings because he seemed indifferent toward spending time with her. However, he had been getting better at it over the past several months, but the last week, he seemed to regress, which hurt her feelings. So, she would begin by saying, "I want to start off by acknowledging how much you have gotten better at expressing interest in spending time with me. I've really appreciated your effort and I have noticed it."

2. Comment on how they may be innocent

The next step is giving them the benefit of the doubt. You may be assuming the worst in their motives and thinking they tried to hurt you purposely, which is very unlikely. Therefore, you must pause and consider all the ways they may be innocent. This doesn't mean they were completely innocent for their hurtful behavior, but it does mean they probably didn't do it with malicious intent to hurt you. Look at their circumstances and upbringing to discern what may have contributed to their hurtful behavior. So, to continue with the example above, the wife could say, "I know this past week you've been consumed with the golf tournament and your brother coming into town and I know quality time wasn't a value you were raised with."

3. Own your part

The first thing to consider is did you do anything that may have influenced your partner's hurtful behavior. For example, perhaps it hurt your feelings that your partner avoided conversation but it's partially because you have a tendency to be long-winded. Also, when we get upset with our partner, it usually says something about us. A great question to always ask yourself is "What does it say about me that I'm upset with them about that?" You may have a sensitivity toward your partner's behavior because it rubs up against a value from your past. For example, if you have a value of feeling heard because growing up you felt heard frequently, you may get particularly upset when you don't feel heard in your marriage because it rubs up against that value. Also, you may have a sensitivity toward your partner's behavior because it rubs up against an emotional wound from your past. With the couple mentioned previously where the husband didn't spend enough time with his wife, her dad never made time for her growing up, which created an emotional wound. Therefore, when her husband seems indifferent toward spending time with her, it activates that emotional wound from her upbringing, which intensifies her reaction. To clarify, even though it's activating her previous wound, that doesn't mean her husband hasn't done anything wrong. It just means her reaction toward his behavior is probably stronger than it would be if she didn't have that emotional wound. Therefore, she could say something like "I know my dad never spending time with me growing up is a wound, and it can intensify my reaction to you not spending time with me."

4. Say your complaint

Now that you've covered steps one through three, you're ready to say your complaint. If you skip these steps and start out with a complaint, you can guarantee your partner will become defensive and comment on how they have gotten better, how it wasn't their fault, and how it was actually your fault. Therefore, if you begin with those three items first, it will make them feel validated, which will optimize their receptivity to your complaint. Now, there are a few guidelines for making the complaint. First, you're not allowed to say "you," because it's accusatory, and you can't say "always or never," because they are generalizations. Not being allowed to say "you" in a complaint can be tricky and may need some extra practice. For example, instead of saying "You never listen to me," you could say, "I rarely feel listened to." Or instead of saying "You never pick up after yourself," you could say, "Things are left out frequently." Also, the moment you say *always* or *never*, your partner will think back to the exact moment when what you're saying wasn't true.

Next, you must identify your tender underbelly under the anger. Anger is almost always a secondary emotion, and underneath it is something tender, such as hurt, sad, lonely, insecure, scared, etc. If you express anger, your spouse will feel attacked and become defensive, but if you express your tender underbelly, it will make them feel more empathetic. Last, identify what core need is getting stirred up for you under your complaint. As mentioned previously, core needs can include wanting to feel heard, supported, connected, adored, prioritized, respected, etc. So, a complaint for the woman in our steps above could be, "This past week, I felt sad and lonely because spending time with me didn't feel like a priority, and it tapped into my core needs of wanting to feel connected and prioritized."

To put it all together, the woman in the example above could say, "I want to start off by acknowledging how much you have gotten better at expressing interest in spending time with me. I've really appreciated your effort, and I have noticed it. I know this past week you've been consumed with the golf tournament and your brother coming into town and I know quality time wasn't a value you were raised with. I also know my dad never spending time with me growing up is an emotional wound and can intensify my reaction to not feeling prioritized. But this past week I felt sad and lonely because spending time with me didn't feel like a priority, and it tapped into my core needs of wanting to feel connected and prioritized."

The complainer steps provide a constructive way to express your complaint, while maximizing the chances of your partner hearing you and feeling motivated to change. Now, this doesn't mean you should start making daily complaints, because then you will appear hypercritical and like nothing is ever good enough. However, one to two complaints per week using the complainer steps is reasonable.

The listener steps

1. 50 percent rule

The first thing to do once your partner is done with their

complaint is summarize what you heard to be sure you understood it correctly. If you don't have the complaint correct, the rest of the steps on how to respond well won't be effective. So, the husband in the previous example would summarize the complaint by saying "Overall you felt sad and lonely last week because you didn't feel like I made you a priority and that tapped into your need to feel connected and prioritized, is that right?" Next, spend time reflecting on the 50 percent rule. The 50 percent rule says you probably can't take 100 percent ownership for your partner's complaint because they may be projecting some of their issues onto you plus you probably had some valid reasons for your behavior that wasn't your fault. However, you probably also can't take zero responsibility for their complaint. Therefore, you're searching for the 50 percent, give or take, you can take ownership for.

2. Ownership

Once you've identified the kernel of truth in the complaint you can own without excuses, begin by making an ownership statement that starts with "I own that I ......" So, the husband who didn't prioritize time with his wife could say "I own that I've had a tendency to not prioritize quality time together and I own that I could have checked in with you more last week." Watch out for the temptation to add the reasons for your behavior you're owning. Doing so will sound defensive and water down the power of your ownership. There's something extremely healing to hear your partner say what they own without excuses. This is also your opportunity to become refined as discussed in Marriage Step #1. Your partner's complaint is probably highlighting a blind spot or growth area for you that if addressed, could make you into a better person and partner.

3. Empathize

Next, provide empathy on how the part you're owning probably made your partner feel. A great empathy statement is "I can see how my behavior of ____ would have made you feel ____." As a recap, empathy is seeing the situation from your partner's perspective. You may personally disagree with how your behavior made your partner feel, but you must consider the emotional wounds and values from their upbringing, their temperament, insecurities, stressors, current values, and marital needs. When considering all those variables, you'll begin to see how your behavior made them feel a certain way, and that's where true empathy comes from. Responding with empathy is like rubbing salve on their emotional wound. If you get defensive, it's like throwing salt in it. So, the husband in the previous example could say "I can see how me not prioritizing our quality time and not checking in with you last week would have made you feel sad and lonely."

4. Apologize

After you've provided ownership and empathy, it's time to make an apology. The apology is only on the kernel of truth in the complaint you're owning so that it's sincere. It can be hard to forgive your partner until you hear them say they are sorry. However, it can be hard to make an apology for something you don't feel like you did. Therefore, it's important to only focus on the part of their complaint you're fully owning and that's what you apologize for. So, the husband in the above example could say "I'm sorry that I've had a tendency to not prioritize our quality time and I'm sorry I didn't check in with you more last week."

5. Make amends

Now that you've taken ownership for your part, provided empathy, and given an apology, it's time to make amends. Making amends is where you suggest what you could do to make your partner feel better. The goal is to provide emotionally corrective experiences to help your partner heal from your hurtful behavior. So, the husband in the example we've been using could say "How about I stop work early tomorrow and plan a special evening for us together, how would that be?" You also want to ask your partner if they have any other suggestions they would prefer. So, the husband would end with "What else would you like for me to do?"

To put it all together it would sound like this, "Your complaint is I hurt your feelings last week by not spending enough time with you and it made you sad and lonely and tapped into your core needs of wanting to feel prioritized and connected. Is that right?" (She says yes then he takes a few moments or longer to reflect on the 50 percent rule to discern what part of the complaint he can own). Then he says "I own that I've tended to not prioritize quality time in our relationship and I own that I could have checked in with you more last week. I can see how my behavior of not prioritizing quality time and not checking in with you would have made you feel sad and lonely. I'm sorry I've had a tendency to not prioritize quality time and I'm sorry for not checking in with you last week. How about I end work early tomorrow and plan a special evening for us? How would that be? What else would you like me to do?"

Once you have finished the listener steps, if you have a complaint to make in response do it using the complainer steps while your partner responds with the listener steps. Keep doing this back and forth until you both are finished. If either of you become flooded at any time during the steps take a break to relax then come back when you both are calm and ready to continue.

Application Exercise:

Practice the reunite tool now while it's fresh in your mind. You and your partner each think of one complaint you want to make about the other and then take turns being the complainer and the listener.

Complainer Steps (go first)	Listener Steps (go second)
1-Progress. Comment on how they have improved over the past 6-12 months on the hurtful behavior that upset you.	**1-Summarize.** Summarize their complaint and ask if it is correct. Consider the 50% rule for the kernel of truth you can own without excuses.
2-Benefit of the Doubt. Comment on how their upbringing and/or circumstances may have influenced their hurtful behavior.	**2-Ownership.** "I own that I have a tendency to ____."
3-Your Part. Comment on how you may have contributed to their hurtful behavior and/or how it may be stirring up a value or wound from your past.	**3-Empathy.** "I can see how my tendency to ____ would make you feel ____."
4-Complaint. Make your complaint without "you, always, never" and express your tender underbelly and your core need under the complaint. "The pattern of ____makes me feel _____ and it taps into my core need for ____."	**4-Apology.** "I'm sorry for how my tendency to ____ makes you feel ____."
	5-Make Amends. "How about moving forward I ____, what do you think?"

Application Question:

What parts of the chapter were most helpful for you and why?

References

Feldman, R. (2020). *Psychology and Your Life: With P.O.W.E.R.*

Learning (4th ed.). McGraw-Hill Education.

Gottman, J. M. & Silver, N. (2015). *The Seven Principles for Making Marriage Work.* Harmony.

Greenberger, D. & Padesky, C. (2015) *Mind Over Mood, Change How You Feel by Changing the Way You Think,* (2nd ed.). The Guilford Press.

Harley, W. F. & Chalmers, J. H. (2013). *Surviving an Affair.* Baker Publishing Group.

Myers, D. & Twenge, J. (2018). *Social Psychology* (13th ed). McGraw-Hill Education Rosenthal, H. (2017). *Encyclopedia of Counseling* (4th ed.). Routledge.

Chapter 5

Marriage Step Five: Cultivating Sexual Fireworks

How to satisfy a low-libido partner:

Caress, praise, pamper, relish, savor, massage, make plans, empathize, serenade, compliment, support, feed, humor, console, hug, coddle, protect, correspond, anticipate, nuzzle, minister to, forgive, sacrifice for, fascinate, attend, trust, defend, brag about, acquiesce, help, acknowledge, embrace, accept, hear, understand, respect, dream of, promise, deliver, commit, serve, rub, indulge, wow, dazzle, amaze, idolize.

How to satisfy a high-libido partner:

Show up naked

Couples always get a good laugh out of that joke when I share it at my Total Marriage Refresh conference, and it certainly is true for many people.

Chapter 5

Before discussing different libidos, let's begin by covering why sexual intimacy is so important for marriage. First, sex is similar to your wedding rings. Why do you wear wedding rings? To symbolize your love and commitment to your partner. Likewise, sexual intimacy is a symbol of your ongoing love and commitment to your partner. Second, it bonds you together emotionally, physically, and spiritually. It bonds you together emotionally because couples often feel more connected during sexual activity and afterwards. It bonds you together physically because skin on skin contact and orgasm releases Oxytocin in your brain, which is known as the love drug. The release of Oxytocin during sexual activity literally bonds you to your partner. It bonds you together spiritually because it's sacred ground. The marriage bed is the only place you get to experience sexual connection so it's special. Third, sex is good for you. Many people know sex burns calories, promotes sound sleep, reduces pain levels, and improves your immune system. We were obviously wired to have sex because it's healthy for both partners!

The most powerful need for most high-libido partners is sexual intimacy, and the most powerful need for most low-libido partners is emotional intimacy. Both need to be understood and respected. Many high-libido partners have said, "All my spouse wants to do is talk about their stupid feelings. How boring!" And many low-libido partners have said "All my spouse thinks about is sex. They're so shallow." Both are disrespectful and dishonoring. The truth is that the emotional intimacy need for low-libido partners and the sexual need for high-libido partners are both valid. It's how they're both wired.

Sex drive is primarily connected to testosterone. The higher the testosterone, the higher the sex drive. However, one's early experiences with sex also impact libido. The more positive the early sexual experiences, the higher the libido becomes, because there's a positive association. Likewise, the more negative the early sexual experiences, the lower the libido becomes, because there's a negative association. One way to think about the sex drive of low-libido partners is like a candle flame. It's there, but it's not very strong, a little flicker of a flame. Therefore, it doesn't take much to blow it out. You're stressed, the flame's blown out. You're feeling distant with your partner, the flame's blown out. You're feeling too busy, the flame's blown out.

In contrast, the sex drive of a high-libido partner is more like a bonfire, a raging force within them. Because their libido is so powerful and sex makes them feel so good, they often turn to it in response to things in life. You're stressed, you turn to sex for a release. You're feeling distant with your partner, you turn to sex to get closer. You're feeling too busy, there's always time for sex.

The libido difference between my wife and me was captured well on our honeymoon. I'm the high-libido partner in my marriage, and when we got to our resort, I couldn't wait to go back to our room to have sex. However, that was the furthest thing from my wife's mind, evident by the following story. On our walk through the resort near the ocean, my wife stumbled upon a little baby crab that was injured. Being an animal lover, she immediately felt bad for the little critter and dropped all her luggage to care for it. The next hour or two were one of the longest periods in my life as she continually talked to it, tended to it, and tried nursing it back to health. She even named it Hermy! As the minutes ticked away, I increasingly made comments like, "Hermy looks fine to me. You've done a great job. I think we can release him now," hoping it would convince my new bride to continue our journey back to our love chamber. Eventually, she released Hermy into the ocean, and we made our way to our room, but I always think back to that story as a clear example of our differences in libido. Sex was the main thing on my agenda, and it wasn't even on her radar.

Application Questions:

Who is the high-libido and low-libido partner in your marriage?

How do those differences impact your relationship?

Some wonder if it's okay for a low-libido partner to say no to sex, or are they supposed to always say yes as part of their marital duty? It's okay to say no sometimes to sex for a variety of factors, such as feeling exhausted, feeling distant, etc. However, problems occur when the default answer to sex is no. When no becomes the predominant culture in the marriage, the high-libido partner eventually stops initiating and emotionally withdraws out of rejection and frustration, making the low-libido partner feel more distant and even less open to sex, which creates a vicious cycle.

Low-libido partners

A lot of low-libido partners complain they don't want sex because their high-libido partner isn't affectionate enough or cherishing enough. If that's the case, try flooding your marriage with sex for thirty days by initiating more sex than your high-libido partner can keep up with, and see what happens. Most likely you'll experience a 180-degree turnaround in your high-libido spouse. They'll probably start doting on you hand and foot, will be extremely affectionate, and will start cherishing you immensely.

One thing to remember is arousal is responsive for low-libido partners. This means you most likely won't feel sexual arousal until after foreplay begins, not before. Therefore, if your partner is interested in sex, don't think about if you're in the mood or not; instead, think about if you're open to getting in the mood after foreplay begins. Also, your brain is your largest sexual organ. Therefore, if you know you want to have sex with your partner later in the day, intentionally think sexy thoughts throughout the day. For example, you can think about what you would like to wear to feel sexy, how you would like to set up the room to make it romantic, or reflect on a passionate memory with your partner from the past. Thinking sexy thoughts throughout the day is a wonderful way to slowly get your brain engaged and prepped for what's to come!

Another key piece for some low-libido partners is working through any unhealed sexual trauma you have that could be lowering your libido. Around one in three women have had sexual trauma, as have roughly one in five men. When someone experiences sexual trauma, they often go in one of two directions. First, some turn hypersexual, where they become highly promiscuous and continually initiate sex to maximize their control, so they are never powerless to sex again. Second, some turn hyposexual, where they want nothing to do with sex and they avoid it because their trauma was so horrible. If you have untreated sexual trauma, you need to receive healing, which usually involves working with a sexual trauma therapist. Your body won't experience arousal unless you're relaxed, and if you have unhealed sexual trauma, you won't be relaxed during sexual activity. Instead, you'll have moments of anxiety and panic because you've experienced destructive sex. When those negative feelings arise, your body will freeze, and you won't be able to experience arousal. If you continue engaging sexually even though you feel panicked, you may get retraumatized. Therefore, if you've experienced sexual trauma in the past and have never received help for it, I urge you to do so. Otherwise, the sexual connection in your marriage will continually be strained.

Case Study: As mentioned previously, my wife experienced sexual trauma numerous times growing up. In turn, she became hyposexual, where she avoided sexual activity in the early part of our marriage because it reminded her of the trauma. When we would be sexual, she would repeatedly get triggered and become hostile toward me. Common thoughts running through her mind were "Sex is disgusting, I'm being used, sex and love don't go together, and I'm powerless." I responded poorly to her hostility during sexual activity and became hostile in response because she was activating wounds from my past of feeling rejected. This set up a vicious cycle that made us drift further and further apart. Finally, as our marriage hung on by a thread, we started seeking professional help, and that began a multiyear journey working with several therapists to heal our crippled marriage. The breakthrough finally came when I realized her trauma surfaced in our marriage because she felt secure enough to process it. And, when she got triggered what she needed was to complete the trauma cycle by being reminded she's safe, no one's going to hurt her, and I'm right here for her. Instead of helping her complete the trauma cycle, I made it worse by getting angry at her rejection, which made her avoid sex even more. The combination of seeing her innocence and my contribution filled me with compassion toward her sexual avoidance I had historically blamed all on her. Her seeing my ownership and sincere empathy broke down her walls toward me.

Application Questions:

Have you experienced sexual trauma in your past?

If so, how has it impacted you?

How often do you feel anxiety and panic during sexual activity, and how much does that impede your experience?

Are you willing to start working with a therapist to heal your trauma?

Another thing to consider is sexual connection for high-libido partners makes them feel adequate, affirmed, loved, wanted, and valued. Nothing hits them deeper at the core than sex, which is why they desire it so much. Therefore, your high-libido partner doesn't desire sex because they're shallow or selfish. Far from it. They desire it because it's the most profound way for them to feel close with you.

Also, high-libido partners usually have a biological buildup for sexual release every two to three days, depending on their age. Their sexual desire is continually building and starts over after every sexual release. In contrast, low-libido partners don't have any type of similar buildup, which is why they can go for extended periods of time without ever thinking about sex. I've had many low-libido partners in my counseling office tell me they'd be fine going for years without sex. Also, libido builds upon libido, so as low-libido partners have less sex, they desire it less, so they have it less, which lowers their desire even more.

If you're a female with a lower libido, your partner may need some sex education to increase your pleasure. The clitoris is the only part on the human body designed exclusively for pleasure. It serves no other purpose! As discussed in the book She Comes First by Ian Kerner (2004), the clitoris is made of the same embryonic material as the penis, it has a shaft and a head like a penis, and it gets larger when aroused like a penis. Also, the clitoral head has over eight thousand nerve fibers compared to only four thousand in the penis head, the outer lips of the vulva are made from the same material as the scrotum, and the protective hood covering the clitoral head is akin to the foreskin covering the penis. Furthermore, the five sensory hot spots of the vulva include the clitoral shaft, the clitoral head, the frenulum, the perineum, and the clitoral cluster. Last, the clitoral cluster is better known as the G-spot and is behind the vaginal wall on the other side of the clitoris, and the vulva is cleaner than the human mouth. In contrast to the highly sensitive clitoral head, the inside walls of the vagina have very few nerve fibers, which is why pleasure for most women declines rapidly when intercourse begins because there's not enough clitoral stimulation.

To pleasure a woman, begin with candlelight and soft music playing. Then, start lightly caressing, kissing, or massaging her for ten to fifteen minutes without touching her vulva, so she has time to build arousal. Caress and kiss her hair, face, shoulders, arms, hands, stomach, legs, and then breasts last. Next, move to the vulva and start on the outside and slowly work your way to the clitoris. Initial activity can include gentle pinches and kisses to the outer and inner lips of the vulva for three to five minutes.

Then, move toward the clitoris and begin experimenting with types of pressure and motion. For example, some women enjoy light pressure on their clitoris, whereas others enjoy firm touch. Where a woman is in her arousal also may influence the type of pressure she desires. Also, experiment with the type of motion applied to her clitoris. Some women like firm pressure with no motion so they can move against it for pleasure, whereas others may enjoy a vertical, horizontal, or circular motion or some combination of all three. Last, experiment with using your hand, tongue, or a combination of both to see which feels best to her. Each woman is different, so be sure to keep lines of communication open on what she wants more of, less of, etc. Continue this activity until she reaches orgasm.

Application Questions:

What's your reaction to the information about the clitoris?

How could this information change your approach to sex?

Five tips for great sex for low-libido partners

1. Make it about you first and foremost.

The first tip is you need to prioritize yourself sexually. This may sound counterintuitive, but I'm giving you permission to be selfish here. The more you enjoy yourself, the more your partner will automatically enjoy the encounter too. In contrast, the less you're into it and just going through the motions, the less enjoyable it will be for both of you. Therefore, think about what it would take to put your needs first during your sexual encounters. What do you need more of, less of, etc. to heighten your arousal and make it an enjoyable experience? The main thing to continually ask yourself is "where do I want to be touched next?" This question will help you tune into your body and let it be your guide.

2. Communicate by saying nah, nnnn, or nice.

Some spouses criticize their partner for touching them wrong. For example, if their partner is rubbing their leg and they dislike it, they respond with, "Stop it! I hate it when you rub my leg." Rebukes will cripple your partner. High-libido partners don't quite know how to turn you on. They're turning knobs, cranking levers, and pushing buttons, trying to see what will light you up. Therefore, if you react with agitation and anger, it will crush them. However, silence is also not the solution, because they can't read your mind with what feels good. So, consider three options to communicate to your partner in response to their touch: nah, nnnn, or nice (The Intimacy Institute, 2015). Nah means please stop; I don't like it. Nnnn means it's okay but not my favorite. Nice means it feels great and please continue. Communicating this to your partner is imperative, so they learn your body map. Your body map includes all the places on your body that feel good to be touched and how to be touched. For example, some parts of your body you may love light tickles, other parts you may enjoy firm massage, and other parts you may enjoy kisses. Experiment. Invite your partner to touch your body one section at a time while they try out different types of touch and you provide feedback with nah, nnnn, or nice. Start with all the nonsexual parts of your body first, and then try it with your sexual parts. Doing so will teach your partner what feels best to you, which will increase your enjoyment during sexual activity.

Learning how to touch your spouse in ways they enjoy is

often a learning curve. I was raised by a mother who was hardy with her touch. She would often pat me on the back firmly or squeeze me tightly for affection. This is my normal. In the early years of my marriage, my wife would often say "you never give me affection" and I would say "what do you mean, I'm constantly patting you on the back and squeezing you tight." She would then reply with "I hate that type of touch. I only want light tickles." Not surprisingly, light tickles are what her mother provided for affection growing up, so that's her normal. So, don't be surprised if you go through a learning curve on how to touch your partner optimally.

3. Please your five senses.

We have been given our five senses to experience the world: taste, touch, sight, sound, and smell. However, we often forget to maximize pleasure in our five senses during sexual activity. Therefore, consider what would bring pleasure to your five senses during your next sexual encounter, to maximize pleasure. What would you love to be tasting? Some couples love to munch on dark chocolate and strawberries during sexual activity. What type of surface and clothing would feel most comfortable to you? Would you prefer soft, silky, rough, cold, hot, etc.? What level of light would be most soothing to you? Would you prefer bright lights, low lights, no lights? What would you like to be listening to? Would you like silence, nature sounds, AC/DC? What would be pleasant to you? Would you love to smell vanilla, coconut, lavender? Maximizing the five senses during sexual encounters will heighten your pleasure and enjoyment.

4. Sympathetic (panic) vs. parasympathetic (peaceful)

nervous system.

We have two nervous systems, the sympathetic and parasympathetic. The sympathetic nervous system kicks in when we sense danger. It puts our body into fight-or-flight and sends alarm bells that we need to be on high alert. In contrast, the parasympathetic nervous system kicks in when we feel peaceful and relaxed. Your body won't experience arousal unless you're relaxed and in your parasympathetic nervous system. However, if you have unresolved sexual trauma, are stressed about life, or have marital discord, your body will go into the sympathetic (panic) nervous system, which will make arousal impossible. The key is to honor your body rather than ignore it. If you notice yourself going into panic (sympathetic) mode, call a time out and do two things. First, practice deep-breathing exercises by breathing in for five seconds through your nose and ten seconds out of your mouth, like you're blowing on hot soup. Do this repeatedly until your heart rate slows down.

When we panic, our breathing becomes short and shallow from our chest, and when we are relaxed, it becomes long and deep from our belly. Once your breathing starts to relax, the second thing to do is to capture and counter your thoughts. Some common thoughts if there's sexual trauma history may include "This is unsafe, I'm being used, I can't say no, etc." Capture these thoughts by writing them down. Next, use the truth table tool covered in the last chapter. For example, if one of your negative automatic thoughts is "This is unsafe, and I'm being used," you could counter it with the following truth statement: "We're two consenting adults within a committed marriage, my partner is loving and devoted to me, and sex is healthy for our relationship." Then, put it together to create a balanced thought with "This is unsafe, and I'm being used;

however, we're two consenting adults within a committed marriage, my partner is loving and devoted to me, and sex is healthy for our relationship." Learning to pause when you feel panic to relax through deep-breathing exercises and capture/counter your thoughts is vital. It's the only way to begin re-associating sexual activity with safety and control rather than panic and anxiety. Ignoring the panic and pushing through the sexual encounter can retraumatize and make you avoid sex even more in the future.

5. Elevate the importance of sex.

Since you have a low libido, sex is probably rarely on your mind. Therefore, you probably don't initiate it, and you probably turn down sexual advances from your high-libido partner. If that's you, consider zooming out and reflecting on the vital role sex plays in marriage. Sex is a sacred activity reserved just for you and your partner, it creates a profound sense of closeness and intimacy, and it's probably the top way your high-libido partner feels loved. Therefore, consider increasing the priority you put on sex by regularly reflecting on how much it could benefit your marriage.

Application Question:

What do you appreciate most about the five tips for low-libido partners, and how could they benefit your sex life?

High-libido partners

High-libido partners should consider themselves in a sexual accountability loop. Your drive for sex is probably high because you have a high level of testosterone and positive conditioning with sex growing up. Sex makes you feel valued, loved, close, and wanted. If you are properly courting your low-libido spouse with regular emotional closeness, effective conflict resolution, quality time, and affection, they will most likely be open to sexual contact. However, if you neglect the courting behavior, your spouse will probably not be open to sexual contact. This is your sexual accountability loop. If you're doing your part by courting your spouse, your sexual needs will probably be met. However, if you neglect the courtship of your marriage, your spouse probably won't be open to sex, which provides a natural consequence. So, high-libido partners, the first thing to ask yourself if your spouse isn't very open to sex is how much have you been neglecting the courtship of the marriage.

Risks with chronic pornography

Pornography is nothing new, but easy access to it is. For decades, if you wanted porn you had to drive to the seedy part of town to the XXX store with your collar up and sunglasses on, hoping no one recognized you. Because of the trouble and potential embarrassment, most people didn't bother. However, today we have a XXX store on our phones 24/7. The three A's of addiction are anonymity, affordability, and accessibility, and porn provides all three. It's anonymous because you can view it without anyone knowing, it's affordable because the majority of it is free, and it's accessible because it's easily found on the internet. Also, porn lights up the same reward center in the brain as crack cocaine, so its highly addictive. It also mirrors gambling with its random reinforcement reward, because occasionally you hit the jackpot with the ideal image or video. Many high-libido partners feel sexually starved in their marriages and outsource with porn. Research is starting to show some clear trends on the impact of chronic porn use (Your Brain on Porn, 2020). First, users have a higher risk for infidelity because porn exacerbates their already high libido. Second, they often have increased dissatisfaction with their partner because no one can compete with airbrushed bodies and overly responsive porn stars. Third, like all drugs, chronic porn users get desensitized and need more novel imagery to get the same high, tempting some to venture into unethical and illegal child porn. And fourth, chronic porn users often struggle with erectile dysfunction because a real person can't compete with the barrage of erotic imagery porn provides. Consuming large amounts of porn isn't a harmless activity, as many believe. It creates some significant risks you need to be aware of.

Application Questions:

Spend a few moments discussing pornography with your spouse. Which risk factors of chronic porn use were you most surprised by?

What should your approach as a couple be toward porn?

Crock-pot vs. microwave

Low-libido partners tend to take much longer to reach orgasm than high-libido partners, which makes sense, since they are starting with a low libido. Think of low-libido partners like a Crock-Pot, where it takes time for them to warm up sexually. Think of high-libido partners like a microwave, where they heat up quickly sexually. Unfortunately, many high-libido partners approach sexual encounters rambunctiously because they don't need much time to reach orgasm. Their approach is often fast and furious, resulting in them reaching orgasm while their low-libido partner has barely started feeling aroused. This pattern typically leads to resentment in the low-libido partner because their sexual needs are often neglected. Frequent orgasm is important for low-libido partners, so they develop a positive association with sex. You may remember learning about classical conditioning, where Pavlov would ring a bell and feed his dog. With time, the dog would salivate by hearing the bell because he associated it with food. Likewise, with sex and reaching orgasm for low-libido partners. The more they orgasm during sexual activity, the more they'll associate it with pleasure. So, high-libido partners must learn to slow down to give them a chance to heat up.

Five tips for great sex for high-libido partners

1. Court your partner like you were newlyweds to have great sex like you were newlyweds.

Sex is often the most frequent early in a relationship when a couple is first dating and newly married. Part of the reason is because the high-libido partner is doing an amazing job courting their low-libido partner. They spend hours with them cultivating emotional intimacy, they continually display thoughtful gestures, they're patient and gracious, they provide continual affection, etc. Because of all this incredible courting they're receiving, low-libido partners are usually open to sexual encounters. Therefore, if you want to have great sex like you were newlyweds, start courting your low-libido partner again like you were newlyweds.

2. Look into your partner's eyes during sexual activity and orgasm.

Low-libido partners usually crave emotional intimacy and connection, even during sexual encounters. Unfortunately, high-libido partners often get hyper-focused on erotic contact during sexual encounters and forget about nurturing the relationship. One easy way to integrate emotional intimacy during sexual activity is eye contact. Eye contact is very intimate and bonding. Therefore, spend some time looking into your partner's eyes during sexual activity and orgasm. Skin-on-skin contact and orgasm releases the neurotransmitter oxytocin into the brain, which is the bonding chemical. You want that bonding chemical directed toward your spouse and providing eye contact can facilitate that. However, don't overdo it by staring into your partner's eyes too long, especially during orgasm as your body is shaking, because you may appear like you're having a heart attack and traumatize them.

3. Make a plan together on frequency, then implement.

The next idea to consider is scheduling sex. Some people hate the idea of scheduling sex because it feels unspontaneous. If you and your partner have equal libidos, then you probably don't need to schedule sex because you're on the same page with frequency. However, marriages with partners who have equal libidos is very rare. Most marriages have a high-libido partner and a low-libido partner and scheduling sex can be very helpful because it places both partners at the same starting line. For example, if a couple agrees to Tuesday evening sex. it provides the low-libido partner time to mentally prepare and it provides the high-libido partner predictability on when the next sexual encounter will occur. Low-libido partners benefit from time to prepare so they can start thinking about how to optimize their five senses during the sexual encounter, which slowly starts to warm them up. High-libido partners benefit from predictability because it provides a sense of control around their top need. One of the hardest situations is when a high-libido partner comes on to their low-libido partner unannounced, making the low-libido partner feel stuck between a rock and a hard place. They can either say no and reject their partner or say yes and have obligation sex. Both options stink! Scheduling sex removes these situations and provides the same expectations for both partners at the same time. If you feel like scheduling sex could help you, there's several ways to approach it. Some couples like to have sex on the same day of the week to keep it consistent, such as every Wednesday—hump day—perfect! Other couples put partner A in charge of initiating anytime Monday through Thursday and partner B in charge of initiating anytime Friday through Sunday. This approach combines some level of predictability along with spontaneity.

4. Ask your partner what it would take to have more sex.

High-libido partners should ask their low-libido spouse what it would take to have more sex. As mentioned previously, I'm the high-libido partner in my marriage, and several years ago, I was wishing my wife and I could have more sex, so I asked her what it would take. One of her responses I'll never forget. She said, "When you let me go out with my friends and you watch all the kids at home, it makes me want to come home and have sex with you." Bewildered, I asked, "How does letting you go out with your friends make you want to come home and have sex with me?" She replied, "Because when you let me go out with my friends, I feel like you're giving me something that means so much to me that I want to come home and give you something that means so much to you." I said, "Okay, from now on you need to go out with your friends every night of the week!" So, ask your partner what it would take to have more sex. You may be surprised at what they tell you.

5. Move slowly to give your partner time to warm up.

Fifth, it's essential to give your low-libido partner time to warm up. We already discussed how most low-libido partners are like a Crock-Pot so approach sexual activity accordingly. Make it a goal to not have intercourse until after the low-libido partner has reached orgasm or is close to it. Doing so prioritizes their pleasure and experience first. Non-intercourse activity can include kissing, caressing, massaging, and manual or oral stimulation. Most high-libido partners rush through foreplay to get to the main event of intercourse. However, for most low-libido partners, foreplay is their main event.

Application Question:

What do you appreciate most about the five tips for high-libido partners and how could they benefit your sex life?

Wedding cake model tool

Now it's time to put it all together in what I call the Wedding Cake Model of sexual intimacy.

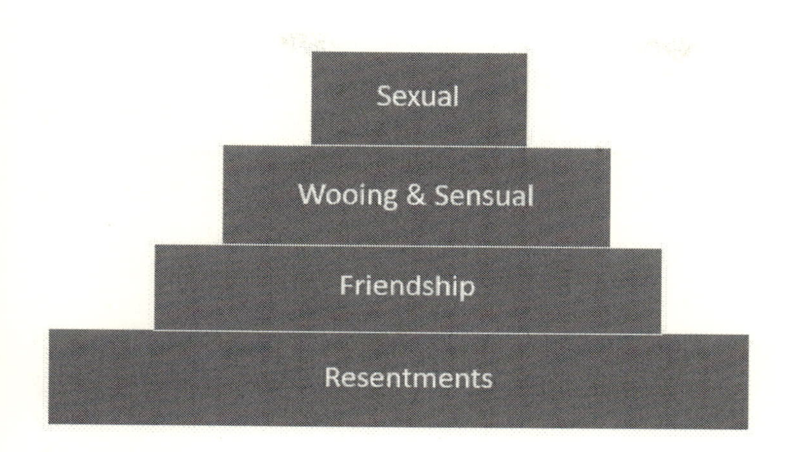

Resentments tier

The base tier is working through resentments. You won't want to have sex with your partner if you resent them and it won't go well if you try. Having sex is like a beautiful plant so you must begin by digging out the rocks in the soil before planting the seeds. Resentments are rocks in the soil of your relationship. They are clogs in your pipes. They block intimacy on all levels. Therefore, resentments must be tended to and resolved first. Refer to the last chapter for ideas and methods to work through resentments in your relationship, such as the compassion chart and reunite tool.

Friendship tier

The second tier of the cake is friendship. This comes second because it's hard to develop a friendship with your partner if you resent them. Nurturing your friendship should be a daily focus but especially during your two mini-dates per week. During your mini-dates, start doing three things. First, cultivate emotional intimacy using the head/heart check covered in the last chapter. Second, cultivate affection, such as holding hands and giving hugs. And third, do something recreational together you both would enjoy, such as hiking, biking, frisbee, or board games.

Wooing & sensual tier

The third tier to the wedding cake model is wooing and sensuality. This comes third because it's hard to woo your partner and have sensual activity together if you don't feel like you're friends first. High-libido partners are in charge of providing emotional wooing sprinkled throughout the week by giving thoughtful compliments, extra affection, and acts of kindness. Low-libido partners are in charge of providing erotic wooing sprinkled throughout the week by flashing parts of their body while changing, rubbing their body against their partner when passing, and sending suggestive texts.

Emotional wooing for high-libido partners and erotic wooing for low-libido partners can sometimes feel inauthentic. Don't push yourself to distress to woo your partner, or else it won't be sustainable. Instead, nudge yourself somewhat out of your comfort zone while starting with the type of wooing that feels most comfortable to you. For example, if sending suggestive texts feels too uncomfortable for a low-libido partner, perhaps begin by flashing some of your naked body while changing. If giving thoughtful compliments feels too uncomfortable for a high-libido partner, perhaps begin by increasing your affection. Your partner wants to be wooed in the top way they experience love. For low-libido partners, it's usually through emotional connection, and for high-libido partners, it's usually through sexual connection.

Next is sensual activity. Sex therapist Dr. Jenny Skyler at

the Intimacy Institute (2015) says most couples completely neglect sensual activity in their marriage. Some top ideas for sensual activity can include taking a bath or shower together, cuddling, or sensual massage. Whatever activity you choose, I recommend keeping your bathing suits or underwear on because this is not sexual time, it's sensual. If you're nude, usually the low-libido partner will feel pressure that things better turn sexual and the high-libido partner will probably get frustrated if they don't. Therefore, keeping your undergarments on during this time is a nice visual reminder that this is sensual time, not sexual.

There are several things to keep in mind during sensual time that were covered previously. First, you want to maximize your five senses with sight, sound, smell, taste, and touch. For example, if you picked sensual massage, you could light several candles for sight, play some soft flute music for sound, spray yourself with your best perfume or cologne for smell, have a bowl of dark chocolate nearby for taste, and use coconut oil to rub one another's bodies for touch. You want to create a full sensory experience. Next, take turns being the giver and receiver. So, partner A begins by being the giver of the sensual massage for ten to fifteen minutes while partner B receives, and then they take turns. Taking turns being the giver and receiver is important because most of us either get so focused on receiving we forget to give, or we get so focused on giving we forget to receive. Therefore, having designated time for each is important. When you're the receiver, practice giving feedback with nah, nnnn, or nice so your partner learns how to touch your body. Finally, track your thoughts and breathing to see if you start feeling anxious. If you do, pause and relax your breathing then capture and counter your thoughts with the truth table tool covered in the last chapter.

Sensual activity should be added to your two mini-dates per week, so they would now include emotional intimacy, affection, recreation, and sensual activity. Having sensual activity two days a week is advantageous because frequency creates freedom. The low-libido partner will feel freedom because they'll feel less pressure that things need to turn sexual since they'll be trying sensual time again during the next mini-date. Likewise, the high-libido partner will feel freedom because they'll feel less frustrated if things don't turn sexual since they also know they'll be trying sensual time again during the next mini-date.

Sexual tier

Once you've both been the giver and receiver for sensual time, several things can happen. First, neither partner feels any sexual arousal and isn't open to getting aroused, so you stop there. Second, the high-libido partner feels arousal but not the low-libido partner. When this occurs, the high-libido partner can pleasure themselves manually in private if they choose to. Third, both partners either feel arousal or are open to getting aroused, so you move into the top sexual tier. Once you're in the sexual tier, there are options that cater to the low-libido partner. Sometimes the low-libido partner may only be open to everything above the waist, so that's what you do. Other times they may only be open to everything manual below the waist, so that's what you do. Other times they may be open to everything oral below the waist, so that's what you do. Other times they may be open to everything including intercourse, so that's what you do.

Once couples have been married for several years, sexual

activity often digresses to intercourse or nothing at all. For low-libido partners, they often aren't up for intercourse so that leads to nothing at all. Instead, sexual activity needs to be approached like a buffet where you can pick and choose different items (above the waist, manual below the waist, oral below the waist, intercourse), instead of viewing intercourse as the only option. All too often, low-libido partners lose their voice and feel they must have intercourse out of marital duty, which turns into obligation sex. When obligation sex becomes the norm, the lower-libido partner feels resentment, and their libido drops even lower and the high-libido partner feels dissatisfied because they are getting their partner's body but not their soul. Therefore, the sexual tier is designed to erase obligation sex by bringing voice and choice back to the low-libido partner, so whatever sexual activity they choose to engage in they are doing so with full consent. This approach also helps high-libido partners because it increases frequency of some type of sexual activity and it ensures their partner is fully engaged during it.

Application Question:

What did you appreciate most about each tier of the wedding cake model of sexual intimacy and how could it improve your sex life?

Application Question:

What parts of the chapter were most helpful for you and why?

References

Kerner, Ian (2004). *She Comes First: The Thinking Man's Guide to Pleasuring a Woman.* HarperCollins Publisher.

Nagoski, Emily (2015). *Come as You Are: The Surprising New Science That Will Transform Your Sex Life.* Simon & Schuster.

The Intimacy Institute. (2015). *Dr. Jenni Skylar.* https://theintimacyinstitute.org

Your Brain on Porn. (2020). https://www.yourbrainonporn.com

Chapter 6

Marriage Step Six: Staying in Love

Falling in love can feel mysterious. We don't try to fall in love; it just happens. We become enamored with our new partner and can't get enough of them. Because love seems like a mystery, if you fall out of love, the idea of falling back in love seems impossible. How could you ever recreate a mystery? If falling in love is an organic whirlwind of fate, then we are doomed if we fall out of love. Or are we? What if we could discern what made us fall in love and repeat it to fall back in love? That's what this last marriage step is all about, taking the mystery out of falling in love so we can sustain it in our marriage long term. Staying in love is the last marriage step, because after working hard on establishing a covenant foundation, owning your brokenness, learning to share power, developing emotional attachment, and cultivating sexual fireworks, you want to sustain the gains. This chapter will show you how.

Falling in love exercise

Understanding love starts at the beginning. Every married person fell in love with their partner for a reason. Therefore, step one is figuring out what attributes you had in the beginning that made your partner fall in love with you. Most of the time, the traits you possessed in the beginning are what your partner continues to desire from you, because that's what made them fall in love with you in the first place. I can still clearly remember falling in love with my wife back in 1995. She was a freshman and I was a sophomore at the University of Colorado at Boulder, and we lived on the same floor in the dorms. To be honest, the first attribute I noticed about her was her appearance. She was beautiful! Long, wavy blonde hair, curvy figure, toned legs, and bronze-colored skin. Hands down, she was the most attractive girl in the hall! As I got to know her better, other traits I observed made her even more attractive. For starters, she had a very calm, peaceful presence about her, which made me feel comfortable. She also had a very nonjudgmental temperament, which made me feel safe. Next, she was extremely tender hearted and compassionate. She also was active and enjoyed skiing, exercising, and other sports. Last, there was a fascinating intrigue about her because she had traveled all over the world. Yep, she was the entire package for me, and before long, I fell head over heels in love with her. Not surprisingly, these attributes are still important for me in our relationship. I still desire her to be attractive, have a calm presence, be nonjudgmental, be physically active, and travel with me. Now it's your turn.

Application Questions:

Both you and your spouse take turns asking the following four questions.

1. What were the top attributes I possessed that made you fall in love with me?

2. Which of those attributes do you still desire?

3. How much do I still possess those attributes?

4. What could I do to develop those attributes more?

Answers to these questions provide rich data. You should now know what attributes made your partner fall in love with you, which of those traits they still desire, how much you still possess those traits, and what you could do to develop those traits further. The ideal is all traits your partner still desires, you still possess. However, that's rare. Most of us change over time and lose a lot of the initial attributes that made our spouse first fall in love with us, which makes it harder for them to stay in love with us. One attribute I possessed in the beginning that made my wife fall in love with me was being fun. Carpe diem was my life motto in those days. I was the quintessential party animal in college. I was the funny one, the entertainer. Everyone looked to me for a good time. One evening I remember leading a group of more than forty students from party to party all night long across Boulder. She fell in love with me being fun and spontaneous. However, with the heaviness of developing a career, paying the bills, and raising children, that fun-spirited young man turned into a serious, driven, and stressed middle-aged man. Yikes, I was making it harder for my wife to stay in love with me, because I had lost a key attribute that made her fall in love with me in the first place. Loaded with this information, I have two choices: I can be defensive and say, "Sorry I'm not the life of the party anymore, but what do you expect, having so much stress on my shoulders all these years has taken the pep out of my step." Or, I can take ownership and say, "I didn't realize how important my being fun was to you. Makes sense you would still desire it. Let's brainstorm on some ways I can bring some of that back for you." You have the same choice. Once you learn what attributes your spouse still desires from you, you can either get defensive or do something about it. Getting defensive will only make it more difficult for your spouse to stay in love with you. Doing something about it will help them fall more in love with you. The choice is yours!

Love bucket tool

Marriage therapist Willard Harley (2011) says all spouses have various needs in marriage, and we can either meet those needs or neglect them. I think of it as a love bucket. We all have a love bucket inside of us, and our spouse is like a faucet filling it up. When we are first dating, our partner excels at filling it up. Before long, our love bucket is full, and that makes us fall in love with them. However, through the years, whether intentionally or unintentionally, our spouse turns down the faucet and only drips water into our love bucket. Simultaneously, they begin doing behaviors we dislike, which creates a hole in the bottom of our bucket and water starts leaking out. With less water going in and more water going out, our bucket gets lower and lower until finally it's dry, which makes us fall out of love with them. Therefore, one of the most important things I help partners discern in couples counseling is what the top things are that fill up their love bucket and the top things that drain it. If we can determine those items and implement it, love buckets can once again get filled, and couples can fall back in love and stay in love.

Case Study: Matt and Cheryl came in for counseling, and their marriage was hanging on by a thread. They had been married ten years and it was a second marriage for both. Cheryl was fed up with Matt's negative behaviors and was not feeling loved. She decided to give marriage counseling a try but really wanted to move forward with a divorce. During the first session, I introduced the love bucket concept, and we sifted through the top things that fill and drain both of their buckets. They took the concept seriously, along with my advice to review their partner's love bucket daily. I continued seeing them for weekly counseling sessions to troubleshoot areas where they needed extra help and they left each session determined to try harder at filling each other's love bucket. Because of their receptive attitude, hard work, and newfound skills, within six weeks, Cheryl said she was starting to fall back in love with Matt because he was learning to fill her bucket. As her bucket got fuller, it made it easier for her to start filling up his bucket too, which motivated him to fill up hers even more, creating a positive cycle. As their marriage counselor, it was remarkable to see them go from brink of divorce to falling back in love within such a short time. The love bucket works.

Fillers

Dr. Gary Chapman (2015) discusses how there are five love languages, and we each desire one or two of them to feel loved. The list of fillers below includes four of his love languages and adds five more. The additional five are common ones I've seen partners desire in marriage. Fillers are all the behaviors you desire to feel loved and satisfied. Fillers can be things your partner did in the beginning when you were dating, but they stopped through the years. They can be things they still do, and you want them to continue. Or they can be things they've never done, and you gave up on it. Bring that item back. The sky is the limit. What are the top three fillers you need to feel loved and satisfied in your marriage?

The next list is not exhaustive but provides some common fillers and their explanations.

Quality Time- This person feels loved and close when receiving your undivided attention.

Affection- This person feels loved and close from non-sexual touch.

Adoration- This person feels loved and close from appreciation and hearing why you love them.

Emotional Intimacy- This person feels loved and close from sharing and hearing inner thoughts and feelings.

Recreational- This person feels loved and close from physical activity together, such as hiking, biking, swimming, etc.

Sex- This person feels loved and close from sexual activity together.

Support My Interests- This person feels loved and close from questions about important things in their life.

Physical Attraction- This person feels loved and close when you optimize your appearance.

Thoughtful Gestures- This person feels loved and close when you provide acts of kindness.

Once you identify the fillers you desire, it's interesting to explore where they come from. For example, growing up, my mother used to take me out for blueberry muffins once a week before school and ask me all sorts of questions about my life. In my young mind, that became an important part of feeling loved, having someone ask me lots of questions about my life, which is the filler support my interests. Not surprisingly, one of the fillers I desire from my wife is support my interests. Most fillers are either how you were loved growing up or how you weren't loved but always desired.

When you start creating your list of fillers, don't feel like it has to be 100 percent accurate. Some people are quick to list off their top three fillers, whereas others need time identifying theirs. Also, expect your list of fillers to evolve for a bit until the three you select feel spot-on for you. And don't be surprised if your fillers change over time as you develop over your lifespan.

Application Exercise:

Pause now and fill in the next chart with the top three fillers you desire from your partner to feel loved and satisfied in your marriage and explain the origins from your upbringing on why you desire each one. The more your partner understands the origin of your fillers, the more motivated they'll become to honor them.

Partner A- list the fillers you desire to feel loved and satisfied and discuss how each one may be connected to your upbringing	**Partner B- list the fillers you desire to feel loved and satisfied and discuss how each one may be connected to your upbringing**

Once you've filled in the top three fillers you desire from your spouse, give them a number on how well they've filled up your love bucket on each item over the past seven days, with zero being the worst and ten being the best. For example, if one of your fillers is affection and you feel your partner did okay on meeting that need over the past week, you'd give them a five. If they were amazing providing affection, you'd give them a ten. If they provided no affection, you'd give them a zero. Keep in mind you're only evaluating what was within their control. For example, if your partner was in bed with a bad cold part of the week, they wouldn't have been able to provide affection, and it was out of their control, so you wouldn't dock points for that. Some people feel awkward giving numbers on their love bucket. However, providing numbers does several things. First, it provides a quick gauge on how loved you felt over the past week. Second, it provides opportunity for discussion on the numbers, which we'll discuss more later. Third, it provides a concrete way for your partner to track how well they are doing as your partner.

Drainers

Fillers fill up our love bucket, and drainers drain it. A drainer is anything your spouse does that makes you feel negative toward them. Drainers create a hole in the bottom of your love bucket, allowing water to leak out. Therefore, if your partner is doing an amazing job filling your love bucket but simultaneously doing a lot of drainers, water won't stay in your bucket. The drainers will cancel out the fillers. Consequently, it's not effective to just track fillers. We must track both fillers and drainers to successfully fill one another's love bucket.

A few things to keep in mind with drainers. First, some behaviors you dislike in your partner may be opposites of your fillers, but don't list those, because then you're tracking the same behavior twice. For example, if you list sex as a filler and sexual rejection as a drainer, you'd be tracking the same behavior twice.

Just like with the fillers, it's helpful to explore the possible origins of why you don't like your partner's drainer behaviors. As mentioned previously, behaviors we dislike in our partner usually stem from emotional wounds or values from our past. For example, you may have a sensitivity to your partner's harsh anger because it activates an emotional wound of your father being harsh growing up. Or, perhaps in your home growing up calm discussion was valued so you have a sensitivity toward your partner's harsh anger because it violates that value. Helping your partner understand the origins of why you don't like each of their drainer behaviors will increase their motivation to honor it.

The next list is not exhaustive but provides some common drainers and their explanations.

Parenting- This person dislikes their partner's parenting style.

Defensive- This person dislikes how their partner does not take ownership for their part in conflicts.

Finances- This person dislikes how their partner handles money.

Harsh Anger- This person dislikes how their partner gets harsh with their anger.

Passive- This person dislikes how their partner is passive in certain areas of life.

Controlling- This person dislikes how their partner doesn't share power on decision-making.

Addictions- This person dislikes how their partner's addiction interferes with their relationship.

Uneven Workload- This person dislikes how they work more overall than their partner.

Sloppy- This person dislikes how their partner leaves their belongings all over the house.

Application Exercise:

Pause now and fill in the next chart with the top three drainers your partner does that makes you feel negative toward them and explain the possible origins from your upbringing on why you dislike each one.

Partner A- list the drainers your spouse does that makes you feel negative toward them and discuss how each one may be connected to your upbringing	**Partner B- list the drainers your spouse does that makes you feel negative toward them and discuss how each one may be connected to your upbringing**

As with the fillers, you must give your partner numbers on the drainers; however, the scoring is opposite. For the drainers, zero is the best and negative ten is the worst. Zero means your partner didn't do the drainer behavior at all, so no water was drained out of your bucket. Negative ten means they did the drainer behavior a lot over the past seven days, so a lot of water was drained out of your bucket.

The goal on your partner's love bucket list is for you to eventually get eight to ten on each filler and zero to negative two on each drainer. When you do so consistently, you'll become irresistible to them! Your current behaviors in your marriage are burned into your brain. Therefore, it will take time to develop new neuronal pathways, similar to a hiking trail. The dominant trail is well worn, and you follow it without thinking, which is your current marital behavior. However, creating a new trail takes time to wear down the grass before it become the new dominant path, which is your new marital behavior. Normally, when couples first create their list and receive numbers, they are doing drainer behaviors much more than filler behaviors. From my experience working with couples, if they are both putting forth sincere effort on filling up their partner's love bucket, it typically takes six to twelve weeks before filler behaviors become frequent and drainer behaviors become infrequent.

Application Exercise:

Pause now for both you and your partner to complete your list of fillers and drainers and provide numbers on how well your partner did on each item over the past seven days.

Partner A- list the fillers you desire from your partner and give them a number with 10 being the best and 0 being the worst on how well they did over the past 7 days	Partner A- list the drainers you dislike from your partner and give them a number with 0 being the best and -10 being the worst on how well they did over the past 7 days

Partner B- list the fillers you desire from your partner and give them a number with 10 being the best and 0 being the worst on how well they did over the past 7 days	Partner B- list the drainers you dislike from your partner and give them a number with 0 being the best and -10 being the worst on how well they did over the past 7 days

Pro tips to consider:

1. Look at your spouse's list of fillers and drainers daily. Make it prominent, such as putting it on your bathroom mirror, computer, etc. Let their list become your daily mission. Just looking at their list daily will improve your awareness and scores by becoming more mindful of your filler and drainer behaviors.

2. Maximizing your partner's fillers while minimizing the drainers is the fastest way to have them fall back in love with you. It's the path to filling up their love bucket and keeping it

full. It's the answer to staying in love.

3. Keeping your partner's love bucket full is the best way to affair-proof your marriage. If your spouse's love bucket is full, it significantly reduces outside threats to your marriage, because they're happy and content within your marriage.

4. Another advantage to the love bucket is it gives you a chance to reinvent yourself in your marriage, because your spouse is forced to look at your behavior over the past seven days. If you've had difficult behavior in your past, it can sometimes feel like your spouse will never think of you differently. However, your weekly numbers on their bucket list is one of the best ways to demonstrate you're changing.

5. Some of you reading this may be in a season of winter right now in your marriage, and you don't have the energy to provide your partner's fillers. If that's you, don't force it. Instead, concentrate on reducing your drainer behaviors they dislike that are making things even worse.

6. When you receive your partner's list of fillers they desire, some of them may not feel within your wheelhouse. For example, your spouse may list emotional intimacy as a top filler, but you may feel deficient in communicating your inner thoughts and feelings. Don't respond by saying, "Sorry, I'm not able to provide that one because that's not who I am." Responses like that will turn your marriage into a prison for your spouse, because you're telling them they will never get one of their top needs met. Instead, respond with, "I'm not sure how to provide emotional intimacy yet, but I'm willing to do all I can to learn how to do it better." That type of response will honor your spouse and motivate them to do the same with your fillers.

7. Never meet your partner's fillers in a way that makes you suffer or else it won't be sustainable and may build resentment.

Instead, always strive toward meeting their fillers in a way that also works for you.

8. Be careful not to counter-blame your partner's drainer list. For example, if your spouse says you're being controlling and you respond with "Of course I'm controlling, because you're passive, so I have to be." You're blaming them for your behavior and not taking ownership for your part. While your partner's passivity may encourage you to respond with control, it's still your choice if you do. Therefore, you must learn to take ownership for how you choose to respond to your spouse, regardless of how they are behaving.

9. Giving and receiving numbers on the love bucket lists once a week is critical. We must be trained on how to love our partner well and the love bucket list provides the training. Consider setting up some type of weekly rhythm for giving and receiving feedback. If you receive your partner's list, barely look at it, and don't receive regular feedback on it, don't expect things to improve. I have all couples in my practice create their lists and provide numbers to one another at the beginning of every session. Marriage counselors can usually only focus on one problem at a time, which makes progress slow. In contrast, doing the love bucket list with a couple addresses twelve areas in their relationship simultaneously and puts the burden back in their court to be working on their marriage between sessions. Then, we can spend our sessions focusing on which items on their list need the most help.

10. Giving and receiving feedback on the love bucket lists regularly will reduce conflict in your marriage, because it provides a format to proactively discuss your needs and feelings. Also, as your love bucket gets fuller, you'll notice patience and positivity increase in your relationship, because

love promotes grace. The opposite is also true. When couples stop reviewing their love buckets and needs start going unmet, conflict increases. The lower love buckets get, the more partners become agitated and emotionally withdrawal.

11. When receiving feedback on how well you did on your partner's fillers and drainers, have the heart of a student. A good student is teachable, they want to learn, and they ask a lot of questions. I've seen many people get frustrated about the numbers they receive, which is futile. How well you think you did on your partner's bucket doesn't matter. Only your partner's experience of you matters. Avoid the extremes of getting defensive or defeated in response to your partner's feedback. Defensive says *it's not my fault, I don't deserve that score*. Defeated says *I can't do any of this right, so why try?* Both responses are toxic and will make your partner feel hopeless. Instead, ask scaling questions. For example, if you receive a seven on affection, ask what an eight or nine would look like the upcoming week. Understanding what you did the past week that earned you a seven is important information but not as important as learning what to do differently moving forward. Unless you get a perfect score, ask how you could improve one or two points per category each time you receive feedback. Scaling questions like this allows your partner to provide concrete examples of what they are looking for, which is vital for improvement.

I believe in the love bucket method so sincerely that I developed an app for it called Keep the Glow (KTG). The app provides a convenient, powerful tool to help you stay in love. Download it today wherever you get your apps!

Application Question:

Chapter 6

What parts of the chapter were most helpful for you and why?

References

Chapman, Gary. (2015). *The 5 Love Languages: The Secret to Love That Lasts.* Northfield Publishing.

Harley, Willard. (2011). *His Needs, Her Needs.* Baker Publishing Group.

Conclusion

So, there you have it, the six steps to marital satisfaction that will continue to transform your relationship lifelong, provided you study the steps repeatedly until you master them. Marriage step one: establishing a covenant foundation covers the covenant vs. contract approach to marriage, the four seasons of marriage, viewing marriage as a living organism, and seeing marriage as the ultimate refinement tool. This step infuses a deep sense of security into the relationship. Upon that secure base, we move into marriage step two: owning our brokenness. Owning our brokenness includes both partners listing their top areas of shortcomings and how they create vicious cycles in their marriage. This step infuses humility into the relationship. Upon security and humility, we move into marriage step three: learning to share power. Learning to share power focuses on accepting your partner as an equal, respecting their preferences, and ensuring you both have an equal voice in decision-making. This step infuses a sense of equality into the relationship.

Upon security, humility, and equality, we move into marriage step four: developing emotional attachment. Developing emotional attachment focuses on building emotional intimacy, healing resentments, and constructive conflict resolution. This step infuses emotional closeness into the relationship. Upon security, humility, equality, and emotional closeness, we move into marriage step five: cultivating sexual fireworks. Cultivating sexual fireworks focuses on sexual satisfaction for both low and high-libido partners, with voice and choice being central. This step infuses passion into the relationship. Finally, upon security, humility, equality, emotional closeness, and passion, we move into marriage step six: staying in love. Staying in love puts it all together by training couples on their partner's top fillers and drainers. This step infuses love into the relationship. So, walking through the six marriage steps will provide security, humility, equality, emotional closeness, passion, and love in your relationship.

Since the steps build upon one another, if you're struggling in one of them, it may be because a previous step isn't in place yet. Therefore, before moving forward, you may need to move backward and properly address a previous step before making headway in a later step. In addition, if you reach an impasse in one of the steps, be sure to reach out for help, whether through websites, books, podcasts, seminars, friends, mentors, or counselors. There's a tremendous amount of marriage resources available, so utilize them. My website is www.drwyattfisher.com and provides multiple resources to better your relationship, including my Dr. Wyatt Show podcast, Keep the Glow app, Total Marriage Refresh seminar, and Relationship Coaching. You also can follow me on Facebook at https://www.facebook.com/marriagedrwyatt or on Instagram at https://www.instagram.com/marriage_drwyatt/ for daily marriage encouragement.

Lastly, view this book as your new marriage manual. The natural drift for all marriages is toward discontent because it entails two imperfect people living side by side, day in and day out. Therefore, we all need constant reminders on how to do marriage right! View this book as a lifelong resource to continually revisit as needed. Right now, the concepts and tools covered are fresh in your mind; however, a few months down the road they will probably get fuzzy. When that occurs, pick up the book and review the steps again. Similar to a cookbook you go to over and over to remember how to cook your favorite meal, use this book as your marriage cookbook, to review again and again on how to do marriage right. Remember, growth takes time, and many of the concepts covered in this book can be challenging; therefore, it will take persistent effort over time before they become your new normal. Don't give up! Let the content covered create a vision on what to strive toward. Somedays you may hit the vision 80 percent and other days 30 percent. That's okay, as long as you are continually revisiting the steps covered in the book to get you there.

Top 6 Marriage Steps:

Marriage Step #1: Establishing a Covenant Foundation
Marriage Step #2: Owning Your Brokenness
Marriage Step #3: Learning to Share Power
Marriage Step #4: Developing Emotional Attachment
Marriage Step #5: Cultivating Sexual Fireworks
Marriage Step #6: Staying in Love

Top 11 Tools:

Brokenness Chart (to promote humility and ownership)
Bullseye Question (to create safe space to share feedback)
Bounce the Ball (to share power on decisions)
Head/Heart Check (to cultivate emotional intimacy)
Empathy Variable Exercise (to cultivate empathy)
Marriage Huddle (to develop teamwork)
Truth Table (to counter false interpretations)
Compassion Chart (to work through resentments)
Reunite (to work through conflicts)
Wedding Cake Model (to cultivate sexual intimacy)
Love Buckets (to stay in love)

Top 3 Routines:

1-Two mini dates per week and within each one include recreation, affection, sensual activity, and emotional intimacy.

2-One marriage huddle per week to get on the same page and review your love buckets during it and use the reunite tool as needed

3-Head/Heart check four times per week and end it with the bullseye question.

About the Author

Looking for a marriage manual? You've found it! Welcome to the Total Marriage Refresh. We spend thousands of hours on education and training to have a successful career but almost none on how to have a successful marriage. No wonder marriage can be so challenging, we haven't received proper training! This book is your new marriage manual. It will walk you through the top six steps needed for marital satisfaction. The pages are packed with practical insights and tools to help you develop and sustain an amazing relationship. I'm a licensed psychologist with a master's and doctorate in clinical psychology, and I specialize in marriage counseling. In addition, I have been married since 1999 and my own marriage has been to the brink of divorce and back, so I help couples from both a personal and professional perspective.

If you enjoyed the book, please leave a review on Amazon so others are encouraged to read it! Also, be sure to follow me on social media and check out my website to learn more about my other resources for couples, including my podcast, app, retreats, and coaching services.

You can connect with me on:

- https://www.drwyattfisher.com
- https://www.facebook.com/marriagedrwyatt
- https://www.instagram.com/marriage_drwyatt
- https://www.youtube.com/c/MarriageDrWyattShow

Subscribe to my newsletter:

- https://unique-maker-1596.ck.page/13acdbbcb4

Made in the USA
Middletown, DE
22 September 2022